FIELDER'S CHOICE

TIM BERTA

CONTENTS

Dedicated to Zachary Herman Arend, David Joseph Betts, Scott Graham Harmon, Cody E. Holp and Tyler LaMar Williams

"The only thing that feels better than winning is winning when nobody thought you could."
-Hank Aaron

BATTING PRACTICE/PREGAME WARMUP

I do not remember anything about March 2nd, 2007, but it is a day I will never forget. When I first began this project, a question ran through my mind: "How do I write a memoir that revolves around the single most life-altering event in my life, when I have no memory of that event?"

The motor vehicle accident I and others were involved in, one which permanently changed my life and the lives of many, will forever remain a mystery to me in some ways. I have tried to pull every ounce of good from it that is humanly possible but also cannot claim the aftermath of the accident isn't an ongoing battle, presenting an endless revolving door of challenges that must be met head on in a variety of ways.

This memoir is structured like a baseball game. This Batting Practice/Pregame Warmup is a prologue. The chapters are structured into innings with the top half of each inning being mostly what happened and the bottom half being mostly personal thoughts and reflections on those events. The 7th Inning Stretch is my mom's inpatient journal entries from my inpatient hospital stay. The epilogue is labeled Extra Innings, and the thank you section is called Post Game Fireworks.

Information and stories from my life and the bus accident come from a multitude of sources and relay happenings I may not remember. All the technical information regarding the accident is based on the official NTSB (National Transportation Safety Board) accident report. Other stories come from personal memories along with accounts narrated by my friends and family.

This book is not meant to capture every individual story, nor is it meant to serve as a recording of every single event that took place during that dark, hopeless—and occasionally triumphant—time. Instead, these accounts are my best understanding of how the motor vehicle accident occurred, and how its aftermath impacted me and those close to me.

At one early point along this journey, I was told as an indisputable fact all further healing for me was done and the window for any more improvement had closed. Imagine working and striving toward a goal for over twenty-two years, only to have that plan ruined in less than 10 seconds.

I am convinced no human alive can accurately put into words or describe all the physical pain, complicated emotions, raw fear, and flat-out grit that goes into experiencing and enduring an event like the one I did. This is my attempt.

I also must state that this book was written not in the spirit of reviving pain or enabling me and others to relive a catastrophic tragedy. It certainly is not meant to be a guideline for anybody's recovery from trauma. Each person's circumstance, injuries, trials, and tribulations are unique. Instead, this book comes from my sincere desire to honor my fallen teammates and to inspire anyone to persevere in the face of almost certain defeat, whatever their specific challenge may be.

˹ST INNING

Top of the 1st
For the Love of the Game
July 1984 - February 2007

A few weeks after everyone had finished celebrating America's independence, on a beautiful, warm day, I was born Timothy Edward Berta, at Flower Hospital in Sylvania, Ohio. My parents brought me back to their trailer in Monroe, Michigan.

That October, Mom and Dad scooped me out of my baby swing and danced with me in their arms after watching the Detroit Tigers win the World Series, beating the San Diego Padres four games to one.

The Berta family started with my mother, Karen, and my father, Rob. For years, it didn't look like my parents would be able to conceive their own child. However, it wasn't until after an appointment with a fertility doctor, they were successful and had me. My parents felt old compared to some of their friends, and their brothers and sisters, who had already started families well before they did, but they felt blessed that God had granted their request to have children. My birth had been a long time coming—after years of praying and hoping that they would be able to conceive, I was finally here.

After hearing some of the language from neighborhood kids and watching how they acted, my parents knew they did not want their children growing up in that trailer park environment. Mom and Dad made a choice. Neither one of them possessed a college degree, but both worked their butts off, sacrificed, and saved to get out of there. Little did they know that all their sacrifice and hard work for us kids would pay off exponentially.

Dad, at that time, was in an advertising business, and Mom in an office job in Monroe. As soon as they were financially able to, they bought a house in Ida, Michigan. And that was where they stayed. The fact that they were able to have two more children was even more reason to be grateful. Following me was sister Trisha, and finally the youngest sister Tonya. We were children who had full, regular, and healthy lives.

The Berta family grew up in Ida, a rural but expanding community, with a total of about 550 students attending the public high school. Our house was about six minutes away from town, and about twelve miles north of the Ohio border. You could say my life was safe, typical, and filled with love.

Because of their influence and encouragement, from very early on, my sisters and I succeeded in many of our pursuits. Tonya and I were into athletics. Trisha was in the school band and a member of Ida's drama troupe. She directed a school play in high school and her successes continued after she graduated —today, Trisha is a member of the National Honor Society for nurses after a great academic career at Lourdes University. Tonya thrived in college softball at Siena Heights University and was named All Wolverine Hoosier Athletic Conference (WHAC) in both softball and academics. Not only did she graduate with academic honors but also broke the all-time Siena Heights University record for stolen bases. She did this

4

despite having fewer games on the schedule than when the record was previously set.

All three of us were gifted in certain abilities, though none of us had—or still have—everything figured out. We also had the usual sibling rivalry, and we still do. What I *can* say is that all three of us deeply loved each other in the way that most family members do. Times with my sisters and family are still some of my fondest—and most fun—memories.

If we played a board game or card game or backyard sport, none of us had any mercy whatsoever on the other. We would play a game in the backyard called Powerball. This game had a set up of three five-gallon buckets and used three beachballs. Boys and girls from the neighborhood would come join us. Three of the guys would be the "gladiators," and three girls would be the "contenders." The contenders would try to drop their beachballs in the five-gallon buckets, while the gladiators would try to stop them by tackling them or knocking the balls out of their hands.

A memory of one instance sticks out. While we were all trying to thwart Trisha, Tonya slipped into the bucket area. I remember I was with the group trying to get a squirming Trisha down and, at the last second, noticed Tonya sneaking in toward another bucket. I dove at her but not before she, in one swift motion, dropped her ball in the bucket and dodged out of the area. All I got was the back sole of her shoe.

Distraction tactics aside, Trisha was remarkably quick-witted and had the reflexes to match. Throughout the years, we would often play a card game called Spit. The goal was to get rid of your hand of cards as quickly as possible. With her light-ning speed, Trisha could easily beat anyone and everyone at the table—even any adult who dared to join in.

All five of us Bertas—our parents and us kids—attended Ida public schools from kindergarten through graduation. We three siblings were active in a local 4-H club. Our participation in the 4-H club strongly shaped us for the rest of our lives, teaching us responsibility and honest hard work—and inspiring in us a love of community.

All three of us raised sheep and rabbits for the Monroe County Fair. We also participated in numerous community service projects. In fact, our 4-H club earned a state of Michigan award for community service. Raising animals taught me responsibility and generated a dogged work ethic and demonstrated that sometimes reaching a goal requires work every single day. 4-H also proved to me, if you sacrifice and work hard, you can achieve great things and be anything you want to be. Mom and Dad had instilled this attitude in me for as long as I can remember.

From their many lessons, I knew I always wanted to go one step above. Of course, we were still human and children at that, so none of us were all that disappointed when we had other stuff going on and "conveniently" had to miss cleaning out the sheep pen.

As a family, we attended a local church—Saint Joseph's, also in Ida, Michigan. Community service and church taught me how important it is to serve and be aware there are people in the world, and even in our own communities, that are less fortunate than us. Despite my parents' best efforts to teach me otherwise and expose me to the big picture, occasionally I perceived myself as the less fortunate one when I saw others with fancier clothes, shoes, or sports cleats. In my mind, if I wanted things like that one day I just had to work hard.

As a result, I viewed any aspect of life as a competition. If I did anything, I didn't just want to be good, I wanted to excel at it and be the best. I always wanted to win and win everything. Obviously, this was not always realistic.

Since I thought winning would make people like you, I tried lots of different things. As a youth, I explored what made me come alive.

In middle school, I made a valiant attempt to play in the band. Yikes. There was no harmony present. I could not carry a tune in a bucket, playing or singing. Let's just say I'm happy I tried it. That adventure in trying new things only lasted for one semester before I realized band was not a good fit. I'm sure the rest of my family was relieved once I gave up band too. It must have been music to their ears when they learned they would no longer have to suffer through my unexceptional efforts to play a coronet squealing throughout the house.

Yes, I worked hard at lots of stuff, but I was just like everyone else and had my own fair share of human moments. I usually did things my own way and rarely followed the crowd, especially if I thought the crowd was wrong. Still, deep down, I really enjoyed being liked and accepted by my peers.

Along these lines, my mother once told me a story from when I was little. I wanted a certain type of shoe that I reasoned would make me "cool," and the "cool" shoes were over the budget my parents had set. I must have made a strong case for why we should purchase them anyway, because my mother, in her telling me like it is practical tone finally told me, "We have only this much budgeted for your shoes. If you want those certain shoes, that's completely fine, but you'll have to pay the difference." Not wanting or being able to shell out that kind of cash, I swallowed my pride and decided to go without the certain type of shoes that had me convinced I'd be popular. That was probably one of my earliest lessons in necessity and reality winning out over luxury.

Still, I did not want to stand out in any way perceived as negative. I saw the way in which having trendy sports cleats or clothes would make me "like everybody else." Yes, I was taught to serve the community, but what other people had or didn't have did not concern me nearly as much as what I felt I had to have so I could be part of the "in" crowd.

Before I began high school, I was enthusiastic about

playing sports and often on a team. Come on now, sports make you "cool," don't they? Even though I wanted to be liked, I really did enjoy playing them and competing. Realizing it was a lot of fun to play sports gave me a direction in life. There are lots of lessons to be learned from sports. Working as a team, sacrifice, the benefits of practice and a big one, playing through pain. You don't always feel the best but if you want success, you must push through. It is also a feeling like no other to be a member of a team, working toward a shared goal.

It made it even more enjoyable once I discovered I was pretty good at them. I was one of the fastest and most athletically talented individuals in school. Catching any ball with my hands and coordinating my whole body in jumping or throwing or swinging required no deep thinking or enormous effort. I soon found in gym class I was one of the first picked for a team along with being "one of those kids" that was highly desired for summer or school teams. Others would struggle to catch or hit or throw a ball and those types of tasks were simple to me. It was so natural that in my youthful mind I did not understand why some had difficulties when I just assumed everybody could do that kind of stuff.

In fact, I have been told a story. Two months before my first birthday dad was playing with me one day in our trailer. Underhandedly he lightly tossed me a small, squishy ball, not knowing if I'd know what to do. I caught it. He tossed it again. I caught it again.

"Karen, you have to come see this." Dad tossed me the ball again. I caught it again. Not bad for a ten-month-old.

So, I was coordinated from early on and catching and throwing anything was natural. Once I discovered this fact, I made the choice to stick to sports. Giving up down time, giving up free time, giving up family trips in August, and in return being sweaty and beat up and tired in sports camps meant a new direction for me. Sports became everything, which only added fire to my competitive nature.

I watched and played baseball before I was even old enough to attend school. I also played football and basketball on the school teams. I was a major contributor in whatever the current sport was in PE, or even when casually socializing and a game was struck up. I remember one time with a lot of guys standing there wanting to get onto the field a football coach saying to somebody, "If you don't get to that spot, I'll find someone who will." I recall thinking, *I want to be the one to get to that spot,* and usually I got there. Being a strong athlete gave me a big part of my identity in school. I had victories early on. Bringing up the early years of my participation in athletics brings about another sports memory.

It was during my seventh-grade year right after the final day of basketball tryouts. I was looking—quite hopefully, I might add—at the list of players who made the seventh-grade basketball team. When that sinking feeling of my best not being good enough hit after reading, rereading and triple checking the list for my name, I knew I had been cut.

I had an earnest ambition, hope and desire to make the team. I mean I thought I was a good athlete! What gives? From my youthful perspective, making the school basketball team was the very definition of what it meant to be cool and would set me apart from many of my peers. This was the earliest point in my life where I remember feeling defeated when it came to athletics.

Once I was picked up from the tryouts that day, Mom saw the devastation in my eyes. After I finally was able to discuss those feelings with her, she gave it to me straight. Mom told me that if I really wanted to be a part of the team, I'd have to figure something else out.

But what? I was out, wasn't I? I had failed. The game was over. I missed the shot.

We brainstormed some ideas and talked about me trying to become a team manager, which I was not crazy about. Mom let me decide, but soon I less than excitedly made the choice to try and become a manager for the boys' basketball team. I approached the eighth-grade basketball coach and asked if he would let me become a manager for the team. Seemingly having no qualms about my proposition, he told me that yes, absolutely I could.

I will admit, in the back of my mind, I sort of wished he would have told me that he was sorry, but the team didn't need anyone to manage it. That way, I (and everybody else) could give myself credit for making the attempt and I wouldn't have to trudge through the duties of being a manager while watching everyone else who made the team out on the court. If the coach rejected my offer to "help out" I would not have to feel like a second-class loser who was not good enough to play—a loser that people felt enough pity for that they would allow him to be a member of the team... but not really *on* the team.

My job as manager did not include wearing a school athletic uniform as I desired. Instead, I found myself wearing a tie and sitting on the bench during both seventh and eighth-grade games. My job was to retrieve and refill water bottles for the players. I was not at all satisfied being a glorified water boy.

Regardless of the massive hit to my little ego, and as difficult as the decision to stick with it was, I endured being a manager for both teams. At the time, of course, I did not see my new position and circumstances in *any* way as a good thing. I was constantly thinking about how demeaning it was to be sitting on the bench in a tie while my friends were on the court playing basketball.

Yes, I was feeling sorry for myself and moping while sitting on the bench during games that season—games that I felt I was missing out on, despite my "participation." Yet, because I was a manager, during practices I was able to mix in with both the seventh and eighth grade teams.

Since I was a manager for both teams, I was present for both practices. When either team would be running drills, I would participate and fill in during scrimmages for both squads. As a result, I get double the practice time—twice as much as I would have if I'd made the seventh-grade team. In addition to the extra practice time, there were hours spent in our family's garage and driveway working on different basketball skills.

I tried out again the next year and made the eighth-grade team. All that hard work paid off. I learned two things—a little humility goes a long way, and sometimes there is more than one way to accomplish a goal. I didn't realize it at the time, but both lessons would become invaluable to me down the road.

Each year, there was a faculty student basketball game in which the eighth-grade boys' basketball team played against a team of faculty members. The seventh-grade coach was one of the faculty members participating. During the game, I received a pass beyond the three-point line. He came out to guard me but not before I drained a three pointer, and the crowd went wild. I may have been wearing the budgeted shoes instead of the fancy "cool" shoes too. So, guess what? The shoes I was wearing did not make any difference whatsoever in forming what would be my earliest memory of experiencing a victory in athletics.

———

For as long as I can remember, I would give my best effort to excel in a competitive sport or school subject—even winning at dodgeball in gym class mattered to me. I set goals for myself and often achieved them in sports or in the classroom.

Soon it was time to enter high school.

A few weeks into ninth grade, I noticed a hallway directly outside our gym. I wandered down it to take a closer look and noticed on one side of the hallway were the athletic awards and trophies. They included track records and coach's awards, or other things related to athletics like different basketball nets and team trophies. I especially took note of the "Most Valuable Male and Female Athlete" for each year since the 1960-61 season. The wall sparkled with the unmistakable glimmer of success, preserved behind glass for all to see—irreversible evidence and validation that winning and being your best self-matters.

On the other side of the hallway and shining in Ida gold on wooden-backed plaques, hung lists of the academic top ten graduates for each graduating class since the earliest year hanging on that wall, 1988. More unalterable confirmation of achievement.

Upon closer examination, I noticed something else. Being a competitor, achiever, and goal-setter, I was curious about those rare students who excelled in everything—meaning, they were both academically and physically gifted. A couple "Most Valu-able Athletes" were there for two consecutive years, and some boys and girls held track records which had been standing for decades, but few, if any, of the students were honored for their achievements on *both* sides of the hallway.

That day, I thought, *Wouldn't it be cool to get on both sides of the hall?* That looked like a goal worth going after, and I figured, *Why not?* I knew it was a longshot because many of the athletic awards had been given specifically for track records, and I did not run track in high school. I chose to be a baseball player. Yes, my chances of getting on both walls were slim, but I was going to go for it, nonetheless.

On the rare occasions I thought about having my name on both sides of the hallway, that fond memory from middle school basketball always emerged.

That winning memory told me not to rule anything out, but I still knew that earning a spot on the athletic side of the hall would be unlikely. In the end, I decided not to worry too much about it and gave everything my best. I simply kept heeding my parents' advice—if you work hard and sacrifice, you can accomplish or be anything you want to be.

There was no real gain I could see from achieving the goal of being honored on both sides of the hall other than a boost to my pride, but, for whatever reason, something compelled me to go after accomplishments. Part of those feelings and what drove me may have come from working nasty, grueling and difficult jobs in the summers. Bailing hay, cleaning camp sites, working fast food, and cleaning public bathrooms were each disgusting and grueling in their own way. I knew for a fact I did not want to do those things the rest of my life.

Maybe it was because I knew I wanted more than what Mom and Dad had. I didn't want to have to worry about finances or budget for certain items. I didn't want to have to worry about anything in life. From my youthful perspective, not having any worries was a possibility if I worked hard enough in school. Sure, us Berta's had everything we needed, but we sometimes had to scrimp and save, and it wasn't always a carefree existence.

Those academic and athletic goals certainly made for some late nights, early mornings, and loss of friend and party time, as well as just down time, but I knew the only way to accomplish something was hard work and dedication.

Over two years had gone by since I first stared at that award wall, and, during my junior year of high school football in the fall of 2001, we were scheduled to play a game against a team from Ohio. The last time Ida High School had played any football team from Ohio was in 1986 against Ottawa Hills High School.

That 2001 season, the team was Evergreen High School

from Metamora, Ohio and the Bluffton University football coaches were in the process of recruiting an athlete from Evergreen. So, they came to Ida High School to observe the game. The offense Ida was running only passed on the odd occasion. I was a starter on defense, but not a starter on offense. I don't remember why but I got in the game on the offensive side of the ball at back-side tight end. We also just happened to run a passing play and our scrambling quarterback threw the ball to me, cutting all the way across the field. I sailed through the air and made the catch in the end zone.

After that game, I received a surprise—Bluffton University had sent me a letter, offering me a spot on their football team. Earlier on in my high school years, I had decided I wanted to become a nurse anesthetist. Due to my upbringing and supportive family, I was almost always thinking about and looking into what I wanted for my future. A fantastic job, in my opinion, would translate into a quality life on other levels.

Science was intriguing, the human body and anatomy fascinating, and it didn't seem there would be many obstacles in the way of getting a job in the healthcare field. Being a nurse would have been fine by itself but becoming a nurse anesthetist seemed like one step above. I chose to go after the next level nursing.

When I received the letter from Bluffton about playing football, it certainly gave me something to think about—as well as a choice that needed to be made. Bluffton did not have a nursing program at that time. I had been considering other schools as well, but I still had the fire of competing and being an athlete. Since Bluffton was an NCAA Division III school, they were not able to offer me athletic scholarship money. NCAA Division III schools are technically not allowed to offer any money for sports scholarships in the way that Division I or II universities are.

Fortunately, due to those years of going after my goal of

being on both sides of the hallway, I had managed to pull off a stellar grade point average. This enabled me to earn substantial academic scholarships. Also, due to my other involvements, I was able to earn different 4-H or community-service-project monies. Once I knew I would be able to attend Bluffton, I was thrilled sports could remain central in my life.

After graduating from Ida in June, I went to Bluffton University in August that year and played my freshman year of football. During that football season, the wide receivers position coach at Bluffton soon gave me a nickname that would stick. Whenever I would run a crisp route or make a smooth catch, he would call me "myboyberta."

Toward the end of that college football season, the Detroit Tigers had accrued one of the worst records in the history of Major League Baseball, going 43-119, and as a result within a couple years, would get a different manager. Bluffton University would need its own new baseball coach my freshman year. Once our football season had finished and the winter snow came and went, an interim baseball coach took over for the coming spring season. As a result, there were few recruits for baseball, and they announced they were having open tryouts.

Though the university had originally recruited me for football, baseball was my first love as far as sports were concerned, so I made a choice and decided to try out. Juggling two sports at the collegiate level—all while maintaining a solid GPA—would be difficult. But being a person who always wanted to go the extra step, I dove in headfirst. I couldn't give up baseball that easy.

I tried out as a catcher, which had been my position at Ida.

I made the team. Many of the positions were already filled by upperclassmen, so I assumed I would not be playing a whole lot. Nonetheless I was overjoyed that baseball could still be part of my life.

I met Bluffton's new baseball coach, James Grandey,

shortly after he arrived. He came in not only as the new head baseball coach but also as the special team's coordinator for the football team. The starting punter had graduated, and the other was injured, so a couple of us who had punted in high school went after the starting punter job. That season, I won the starting role of punter in addition to playing wide receiver. Since Coach Grandey was the football team's special team's coordinator, I worked with him often before baseball season even began, as punters are members of special team's units on football teams.

He was certainly the most animated special teams coach I've ever had. During practices, he would start yelling, "Special teams!" when we were supposed to get on the practice surface. He would be holding the football high above his head at arm's length while sprinting out and slamming the ball down at midfield, keeping it under his paw as the ball hit the ground. Our players could not help but feel his energy and passion. Having a quality special team's unit is imperative for a winning football team. He only helped coach two seasons of football and one of those seasons was the best record of my time playing football there going 5-5.

A side note, in case you're curious... Yes, I won the job of first-string punter but got favorable rolls expanding the distance of my kicks when I punted. I was nothing too special. After being a wide receiver and punting, the other punter returned, and I went back to full-time wide receiver.

I had no plans to quit playing baseball just because there was a new coach, so went out again sophomore year. Even though I was giving everything my best, it soon became obvious playing football and baseball was too much. I was not talented enough in either and needed to spend much more time on just one of them to become as successful as I desired.

I also realized I was not going to be a professional athlete. I was not that good. Playing two sports, working a campus job, plus taking a heavy load of biology classes was not a good choice. It quickly became no fun, and my grades were starting to suffer. The fact that I had no time to do anything besides eat, sleep, hold a campus job in food service, and keep up with all the sports and schoolwork... Well, it turned my college life into one big chore.

Being pulled in so many directions was making me anxious —I knew it was not a good idea to attend a basketball game when I had studies I could be doing, and vice versa, because when I was studying or working, I felt like I was missing out on fun events or winter sports games with friends.

It felt like the "prime' college years of my youth were flying by and all I had to look forward to was the rat race of getting older. Life wasn't one big party—I understood that— but being away from all my friends all the time did not seem like a good trade off. Playing two sports in college seemed like I had made the wrong choice, at least in those moments.

If I feel something, or anything is worth doing, then I go after it with my whole heart. Again, I had a desire to excel. With too much on my plate at once, I was simply not able to go after anything with my whole heart. Just like everybody else, I wanted to enjoy life too. After much agony over the decision, I made a choice. Even though I always wanted to go one step above, I knew one of the sports had to go.

It was comforting knowing I had a hit, made at least one out on defense, stolen a base, and scored a run in an official NCAA baseball game. I also caught a pass and scored a touch-down in an official NCAA football game. I reassured myself with the fact that at least I had given playing two sports in college a shot.

The school had originally recruited me for football, and I enjoyed playing football more. This was confirmed after I realized the weather during most of the football season was much more tolerable than weather during most of college baseball season in Northwest Ohio. On one occasion during my sophomore year, I remember shoveling snow off the baseball field before our home game. With all this in mind, I chose to continue playing football.

Toward the end of the 2005 school year, after baseball season was over, I was walking out of the cafeteria and headed back to my dorm room. As I walked through a building on campus, I remembered Coach Grandey's office was downstairs so I should probably pop in and have a talk with him about my plans.

I thought the decent thing to do would be to go in and tell him of my decision to stop playing baseball. Another part of me thought I could just go to my room and not show up next year for baseball and he would figure it out eventually. I wrestled internally about telling him and possibly disappointing him or myself. The lump in my throat and hole in my belly escalated as I came closer to his door. Telling myself things like, *What are you doing? You're not a quitter. You don't play much anyway, but since when has failure stopped you? If you do this, you're not as special as you think you are and no better than anyone else."*

As Coach Grandey's office neared, memories of baseball filled my head. First off, I had never met someone like coach Grandey. He coached the game of baseball with knowledge, intensity, and zeal. He was just as passionate coaching baseball as he was coaching football. I had memories of countless awesome times over the years of baseball, wonderful teammates, great moments of camaraderie and success. Hitting a walk off triple in high school to win the varsity baseball game after the hitter ahead of me was intentionally walked, throwing out many runners stealing in high school and college, running bases, stealing bases, crossing home plate from little league through college—the list went on and on, like a happy thread of snapshots connecting all my years of baseball. Sunny, warm days, catching pop ups, playing catch in the backyard with my dad or friends until winged bats started chasing the ball and it was too dark to see. I owed a lot to baseball.

Knowing I would never have those moments again was dismaying. It all almost made me stop and turn around. Then I thought about the freezing cold games, the very early mornings and the very late nights and getting hit in the mouth by a baseball (which was totally my fault) all at Bluffton. All that and my grades were suffering. With those details in mind, I knew what needed to be done.

Backtracking and taking the time to have a sit-down with the coach may have meant less time for video games—ahem… I mean, studying—but it would give me some closure on that chapter of my life.

I had to stop for a moment and take a deep breath. I knocked and, after Coach Grandey invited me in, I sat down and thus began one of the most difficult meetings of my life.

"Coach," I began, unwilling to launch right in, "it's good to see you."

With his eyes slightly narrowed he quizzingly replied, "It's good to see you too. What's up?"

"Coach, I don't think I'm going to play baseball anymore. It's just too much and it doesn't seem wise to continue."

"All right, but you have terrific baseball game intelligence and I loved using you for a pinch runner. I could always count on you for a stolen base. I'm going to miss you. Well… Hold on a sec." He shuffled through some papers on his desk. "Ah, here it is. The university allows me one student assistant coach —if you'd be willing or able to do that. You would assist me in practices, games, and travel with the team. You could still lift and run for football but remain a part of the baseball team."

He had just made me an incredible offer. I stared at him in disbelief.

"Does that include going to Florida?" I asked, my voice hopeful.

"Yep."

"Awesome!" My heart filled with joy and anticipation, delighted at the benefit of going to Florida over spring break. "Do I have to decide now… When do you need to know by?"

"You can have a couple days, but if you don't take it, I'll have to find someone else. I need to know soon here."

The thought of dumping my present campus job in food service and working as an assistant baseball coach instead was a dream come true. After what didn't require a huge amount of consideration, I made the choice to join the baseball team as a student assistant coach for the next spring. Football would be my priority. When available, I would still attend baseball practices, games, and travel with the team on their annual spring break trip to Florida, all while being paid. Best of all, baseball would still be part of my life. I left the coach's office that day feeling great about my future.

I had no idea how much that simple choice would forever change my life.

———

Bottom of the 1st
Personal Reflections

Obviously, I don't remember watching the World Series from my baby swing, but that's still cool—symbolic to me—being "introduced" to baseball at such a young age. The object of the baseball game is to win, so I don't know exactly where my competitive drive came from. It was probably a combination of a lot of events and people. I remember observing Mom and Dad working extremely hard around the house and getting up to go to work daily, so I had a great example to watch and learn from. Still, there was a choice to be made in terms of whether I wanted to follow their example of striving or not. I chose to follow their lead.

While growing up, I remember usually endeavoring for greatness in whatever I was doing, be it any type of game, a sporting event, schoolwork, or even a household chore. I admit, with household chores the goal was often to get it done as quickly as possible, but the point is I always wanted to win.

Success came best through hard work, and part of this lay in me knowing that nobody was going to do something for me or give anything freely without me also contributing. My parents certainly did not do everything for me and allowed me to attempt different tasks entirely on my own. That way, I could learn from my choices and experiences. In many areas, they also held me accountable, both rewarding and disciplining me. Reflecting on that fact now, I am grateful.

This brings to my mind a story from my younger years. Apparently, I was three-years old and at a large gathering where lots of extended family were seated around the kitchen table. Everyone was busy eating and chatting. When I asked if I could get a drink of soda pop, Mom, in her typical way of letting me do things for myself, said, "Yes, you know where it is."

The container of soda pop was up on the counter. I would have to reach my arms up above my head to grab it and bring the heavy canister over to the table. To a three-year-old this massive box was heavy and bulky. Upon managing to safely bring the carton down from the counter and over to the table, I now had a different issue. I would have to figure out how to undo the clip and pinch the spout to pour from this unfamiliar container. The weight of it would shift as I was pouring. Since I was so little, I wasn't sure how to manage this. I stood there at the table, contemplating how I was going to get at this stuff without dumping everything.

My extended family saw my problem, and all began to move at once to help, but Mom held her index finger to her lips and waved them off. After a few minutes, I figured out how to open the container and the smoothest way to pour the soda pop while keeping my drinking glass standing. Once finished, I heaved it back on to the counter without spilling even a drop.

Mom had let me problem-solve, thereby allowing for the possibility of failure. This small act—along with many others—empowered me from early on without even realizing it. I knew I could face a challenge and succeed. Neither one of us knew how valuable that seemingly insignificant lesson would turn out to be.

Mom and Dad gave us kids vital lessons we were going to need in the world. I found out later, when Karen and Rob were struggling and saving to get out of their trailer before my sisters were born, they made sure I as a baby had the proper nutrition and nourishment, even when it meant they would have to go without. That is true love in the form of commitment and sacrifice. I had no choice as to who my parents were, and God tremendously blessed me. Thanks to Mom and Dad, I did have a choice about my own effort and dedication in life.

To this day, I am incredibly proud of that commitment and perseverance, and for many reasons. After my senior year of high school at Ida, I was voted the Most Valuable Male Athlete in the school and ended up graduating top ten academically. I succeeded in being honored on both sides of that hallway.

Along with striving for greatness in many things, I remember being upset when things appeared to be unfair, or somebody was being consistently bullied. This wasn't limited to bullies in the form of people.

While my sisters and I were walking our sheep to exercise them before showing at the Monroe County Fair, one of my sheep, for some reason, decided to headbutt my youngest sister, Tonya. He would only headbutt her and no one else. I realized that it was because she was the little one—and thereby the most vulnerable—and this upset me greatly. Because my sheep would only do this when he thought I wasn't looking, I viewed him as a coward. This behavior continued for some time—no matter what I did to discipline or teach him, he continued to go after Tonya.

My sheep was powerful and solid. He outweighed Tonya by at least fifty pounds I was maybe fourteen years old, making Tonya right around eight. I resolved to put a stop to this and protect Tonya. This action was neither easy nor automatic, but I had made a choice, and I was determined to follow through. Every other option had failed to make a difference, so I knew I had to be creative. In the end, when we exercised our sheep, Tonya or I were always first or last, with Trisha walking between Tonya's lamb, Marshmallow, and my lamb, King. It worked. The headbutting from that bully stopped.

On a somewhat funny side note… I had named that lamb "King" before I knew what his personality would become. He certainly grew into the name, but he was the bad sort of king, a tyrant, in fact.

Another time, during high school, there were two students who would bully a younger classmate in the hallways and in the cafeteria. The day I had decided to step in, it had been consistent long enough. I was fed up with the injustice and made a choice.

I walked up to where they were taunting him in the cafeteria line and told the bullies, "Come on, guys—leave him alone. He's not doing anything to you." I was assertive and stayed cool and collected—and they listened to me.

Years later, that bullied student reached out and told me how much it meant I stood up for him. He said he was touched because he knew I didn't have to act but did—and he has never forgotten the gesture. I didn't think much of what I did at the time—it seemed the natural and human thing to do, something anyone would do—but now I can see how impactful it was.

Again, I was nothing special. I was just like any other young boy. I had my stubborn moments, like any child. I did my own fair share of stupid and reckless things. I'll limit the examples, but here is one such illustration. In my youthful mind like most everybody else I thought I was invincible. There were no thoughts about my future either, I mean nothing could ever happen to me.

A group of us guys in high school began to ride and screw around in a beat-up old car on a back dirt road. We were too cool to wear seatbelts and drove as fast as we could over a steep railroad crossing kind of like a ramp. The car sailed over the sharp embankment and thumped onto the road on the other side. No seatbelts meant that us boys inside hit our heads and were knocked around a bit—beat up a tad, sure, but nothing serious. That choice to be reckless in that instance turned out fine. I often continued my wise choices in school and life in general. Well, usually . . .

During my time at Bluffton, my friend, Mike Smith, wanted to ride a bull for his twenty-first birthday. I heard about his desire to do this and, feeling "helpful," wanted to get him ready, or as prepared as I could.

So, we found an old dresser in storage that no one was using. With Mike riding it like a bull, and as violently as I could, I shook and rocked the dresser in the dorm hallway. We probably should not have dragged that dresser out. He could have easily been more seriously hurt than he was, and I was also hurt when, after one particularly rough shake, the dresser landed on my toe. I felt accomplished though since Mike did not fall off the dresser. Much to my disappointment, he only lasted two and a half seconds on the actual bull, so my "training" may not have prepared him as well as I'd hoped . . . We did not get reprimanded by the RA either, who happened to be part of it. There is a video of this in the notes.

Another evening at Bluffton, us guys decided to make some harmless mischief. From a position hidden from view, a couple of my dormmates were loading and launching water balloons at unsuspecting random victims on the campus sidewalk—they also did this a few times at large gatherings. I would hang out near the targets, pretending to be in a phone conversation and not knowing anything of what was about to happen.

I was on the phone with those dormmates telling them where each balloon launched was landing. When the balloon would land, hitting our targets or landing so close to them that it splashed their feet, I would act surprised and look around in bewilderment.

There are other evenings at Bluffton I'd rather not state, but this instance I will mention. I participated in the freshman football thong run, kind of a "football freshman rite of passage" tradition. The freshmen on the football team would wear donated thongs from women or other feminine underwear and run around a dorm building with all the college females watching. Not the best idea either, but I was a freshman trying to fit in and be "one of the guys."

My dumb and all-too-human moments lasted all throughout my life. I was not above doing many careless things and did not always make the smartest choice. Think of all kinds of dumb, reckless, and silly things that almost everybody does as a youngster, and I probably did, or at least was around or considered doing, most of them.

Yes, I had—and still do have on occasion—some less-than-favorable moments. Reflecting on my early years now, I was truly blessed and usually made the right choices. I had two parents who were there for me, loved me, prayed for me, and cared enough to go to work every day so that I and my sisters could have enough food to eat, clothes to wear, and live in a safe environment. Mom and Dad believed in all of us siblings, and all three of us knew they wanted to support us in anything we put our hearts into.

Still, Mom and Dad could never have predicted the path I was ultimately set on.

The combination of unanticipated events and how they came together still blows my mind: Ida High School had not played a school from Ohio in football for sixteen years. When they finally did, I happened to have a good game receiving, even though our offense did not pass the ball often. It was a rare day indeed. Also, the Bluffton scouts were looking at an Evergreen player to recruit, yet they recruited me.

Looking back on those happenings and seeing how they all worked together is remarkable. It's like those times, along with some of the choices I had made early in life, had led and allowed me to attend Bluffton University. It seems like it was meant to be, and not solely based on my efforts. Come to find out, there were grander tasks and much more challenging projects in store for me, about which I knew nothing.

2ND INNING

Top of the 2nd
The Accident
February 27 - March 2nd, 2007

During my senior year at Bluffton University, in 2007, our spring break was scheduled to take place the week of March 5th. Our baseball team bus left Bluffton University in the evening on Thursday, March 1st, for our spring training trip. Because of the distance, it was going to take a few days to drive down to Florida, where we were going to play our games. I was traveling with the team as student coach.

Tuesday evening of the week we left, I was with college buddies in Findlay, Ohio. It was our weekly "guy's night" Fricker's outing for their chicken-wing special. My dad had decided to join us since these Tuesday night chicken wing special events were dwindling with most of us being seniors and eight weeks away from graduating. Dad drove all the way to Findlay from Ida, Michigan for the occasion. He had met me earlier that evening in Findlay to purchase a small device I would use to play music on the trip. As the evening ended at the restaurant, and we hugged goodbye, Dad told me he was so glad we were taking a bus for our spring baseball trip, and not a group of smaller vehicles as the team had done in a previous year.

My freshman year, the Bluffton University baseball team carpooled to Florida with parents of team members who rotated driving.

Being my logical, practical, and realistic self, I had replied, "Well, Dad, a bus can get in a wreck just as easily as a car can." I remember being in Fricker's parking lot and giving him a hug and saying those words before going our separate ways.

I would remember nothing else for months.

In the moments just before the accident the Bluffton University baseball team's bus was passing through downtown Atlanta, Georgia on Interstate 75. It was around five o'clock in the morning on Friday, March 2nd.

From everyone's best guess and from witness testimony, the driver must have thought he was in a High Occupancy Vehicle (HOV) lane. It turned out that the lane was not an HOV lane but was in fact an exit ramp on the left side. Our bus shot up the exit ramp at highway speed. At the end of the exit ramp was a stop sign, and to the right was an overpass that bridged across I-75.

By the time the bus driver realized his mistake, it was too late. He tried to turn a hard right, but we were going too fast. The bus ran through the intersection, hitting the overpass wall. It ramped upward, spinning a full 180 degrees, and plummeted onto the interstate below, landing on its side.

There were thirty-five passengers total on board, including the bus driver and his wife. There were four coaches and one student manager. The other twenty-eight aboard the bus were players on the team. Some of them must have been awake and aware enough of what was happening to grab onto seats in front of them right after the bus collided with the overpass barrier. They stayed inside the bus. A few of the players and coaches were ejected immediately and landed on top of the bridge.

I was ejected after the bus launched over the bridge guard rail and landed on the pavement below.

To put it visually, if the bus landed at the center of a clock face, I landed at two o'clock.

Zach Arend, another player, landed at three o'clock.

I will not get into the graphic details of the deaths. I have heard and read conflicting accounts about some, and out of respect I do not want to say more about one or get anything wrong. I will only say that David Betts, Scott Harmon, Cody Holp, and Tyler Williams were killed at the scene, along with the bus driver and his wife.

Based on the official NTSB (National Transportation Safety Board) accident report, they believe I had been seated approximately in the middle of the bus closer to the back, on what would be the passenger side of a car. The time was 5:38 in the morning.

I have no memory of what exactly happened to me and have heard differing reports from talking to a few of my teammates that were with our group on the bus that day. I'll just give my best guess based on knowing myself.

I was probably stretched out with my seat somewhat reclined, attempting to get a little sleep. This was made easier because there were no seat belts. It's not like me to be able to sleep anywhere except a silent, pitch-black room so I doubt I was fully asleep. When the driver yelled, "Oh, shit," and the driver's wife screamed, I probably heard it.

I'm speculating I did not have any time to react before the bus hit the overpass wall. I'm guessing I was then thrown into the metal ceiling or one of the metal poles that were located inside the bus and knocked out cold. Once unconscious, I was thrown around inside the bus along with other teammates. One writer described us as being tossed around inside the bus "like socks in a dryer."

At some point, I was thrown out of a window, but of course, I have no idea exactly when. I'm guessing my body was limp as I slammed onto the pavement. The fact that I was limp, rather than tense, may have helped make my injuries not as severe as they could have been. I have a strong suspicion I landed on my left hip because years later, a large nugget of glass came out of that hip. If the body cannot digest or destroy a foreign object in the body, it will gradually push the object to the surface.

Again, all of what happened to me is merely guesswork, and I will never know exactly. The Atlanta doctors also can only speculate what precisely happened.

Everything resembling upheaval took place at the accident scene. Another assistant coach told me he was asleep, then an intense jarring and what felt like an explosion launched him into the air. Upon opening his eyes, this same assistant coach soon realized he was laying in the middle of a road on top of a bridge.

After gathering his faculties as best he could, he crawled to look over the edge of the overpass. To his horror, he beheld the bus he had just been riding in laying on its side on the freeway below.

I also heard a story about a group of heroic players. After the bus landed on the freeway below the overpass, they climbed out with minor bumps and bruises. Hearing screams, they all together lifted an edge of the bus just enough to free another survivor's leg who was trapped underneath the wreckage. I don't know who they were but do know I am proud to say those guys are my teammates.

The paramedics and first responders at the scene made the choice to bring me into the hospital even though my score on the Glasgow Coma Scale told them there was little hope.

The Glasgow Coma Scale (GCS) is the most common scoring system used to evaluate the level of consciousness in a person following a traumatic brain injury and is used to help gauge the severity of a brain injury at the scene. A score on the Glasgow Coma Scale is the total of three separate tests. These tests include eye opening response, verbal response, and motor response. A score of 1 on any of those three tests is the lowest, and a score of 5 on each test is the highest. A score of 0 is not used.

In general, a mild injury would be a 13-15 on the scale and a moderate injury would be a score of 9-12. Anything 8 and under is considered a severe brain injury. The paramedics at the scene scored me a 3. Usually, paramedics do not transport anyone scoring less than a 5 on the scale, because they'll be dead within a short amount of time and the effort would be a waste of time and resources.

I do not know what they scored Zach Arend, but I assume we were both about the same.

The paramedics spoke to my parents afterward about bringing Zach and me in. Regarding me, one of the paramedics said, "We scored him a three. We were close to leaving him out there and declaring him dead. He and Zach were both still barely alive, but young and in shape. Those were big reasons we decided to give them a chance." Had these first responders followed the typical procedures, I would have died right there on the pavement. They gave me my very life back, or at least my life as I know it today.

There were many factors during the minutes immediately before and after the accident that made a difference in the outcome.

First responders arrived on the scene within four minutes of the crash to give aid. If you've ever been to downtown Atlanta or any other large, congested city, you would know getting anywhere in four minutes during a typical workday is virtually impossible—and that the blaring sirens mean nothing if there's nowhere for traffic to move.

At the time the accident took place, 5:38 a.m., there was hardly anyone on the roads so that issue did not exist. The paramedics also told my parents that, had the accident happened fifty miles north or south of where it did, they would not have been able to remove my spleen before I had bled out.

Another major factor was that one of the best trauma hospitals in the United States happened to be directly off that freeway. Grady Memorial Hospital is a Level 1 trauma center—a Level 1 is where patients with the most severe trauma injuries are taken and treated.

Adding to all of this, Grady Memorial was double staffed because the night shift hadn't left, and the morning shift had already arrived.

After trauma surgeons removed my spleen, they began a general injury scan, starting at my head. Once they got to my neck, they rushed me to surgery. Any other possible injuries would be insignificant if the issue they had just noticed was not immediately taken care of—they had discovered my brain was immensely swelling. If they didn't perform surgery right away, I would die.

A piece of my skull was removed to give my swelling brain a place to go. They froze this section of skull so they could reattach it if I lived long enough for the swelling to go down.

All this repair work took place while my family back home slept soundly, minutes away from waking to start what they thought would be a routine day.

Moments from the beginning of a day that turned out to be anything but routine. While I stayed tucked away in a dark place.

———

Bottom of the 2nd
Personal Reflections

For a variety of reasons, this reflection was especially difficult to write.

Teammates were killed, yet I remember nothing. There was death and pain and suffering. I remember nothing. There was panic and fear. I remember nothing. There were lifesaving decisions being made. I remember nothing. There was courage and compassion. I remember nothing.

I do remember telling Dad goodbye in Findlay Fricker's parking lot. I remember saying a bus can get in an accident just as easily as a car. To this day, I get a bit spooked by those words. I was just being realistic in terms of how life works, and how could anyone predict a catastrophe like that anyway?

I know what happened to me. I know where I was and my injuries because family and friends who were there informed me, but I have no memory of that time. I often wonder exactly what I was thinking and what I was doing when the bus smashed through the guardrail. How much pain was I in following the accident? I am going to safely assume I was in quite a bit of discomfort after being thrown out of a bus flying off an overpass going freeway speed.

Many of my teammates who survived had far fewer physical injuries, but they do have memories that will haunt them for the rest of their days. I'm glad I don't have those memories, and I feel for them.

But whether I remember or not, the event happened, and I must deal with the consequences. There were years of desperation, hopelessness, and a mountain of a fight to become as functional as I possibly could, given my newfound vast limitations. The worst and most damaging consequence of all is that teammates were killed that day, individuals who I'll never speak to again on this earth.

Yet, without these experiences, I would not know the power of prayer. I would not know the absolute miracles I have been told about or witnessed and experienced firsthand. I would not have met all the wonderful people that assisted and supported me throughout my recovery. I met them under the most heart-breaking circumstances, but the opportunity to get to know them and experience their kindness is an unexpected blessing.

I also have witnessed my impact on people, and it is comforting and inspiring to know I have made a positive impact. Individuals have told me stories I had forgotten, perhaps to remind me of who I was and still could be, when I was struggling with my recovery.

One example is a story from my youth that my parents reminded me about. I would have otherwise forgotten this. It happened when there was a guy bullying a friend of mine while we stood in a lobby in school waiting to be picked up. He had been doing this for the entire time we had been waiting there. Finally, it had gone on long enough and I told the bully to back off and leave my friend alone. The bully stepped back. It appears many of my experiences and actions that came before the accident had been impactful in numerous positive ways.

From what I remember and have been told, my life was going in a good direction, but I wanted more out of my existence and was working toward that. I was always striving for more. I was one step closer to the plan I had been dreaming of ever since my sophomore year of high school. I planned to become a nurse anesthetist and raise a family in a terrific neighborhood and enjoy a tranquil, active, and productive life. Like anyone else, I was looking forward to enjoying all the fruits of my labors.

That said, nothing goes entirely according to plan. My senior year at Bluffton had already not gone exactly as intended. I had badly injured my left shoulder in the first foot-ball game of my senior year and had thereby missed the rest of the season. That ripped my heart out with my other football history at Bluffton.

After not playing much as a freshman since I was an underclassman, I was looking forward to improving and being given a chance as a returner. Then, during my sophomore year, I had to enter football camp with a sprained ankle that came from a meaningless pickup basketball game in Ida that summer, and I ended up missing a portion of that season—the most important early part of the season when your team is developing its "personality" and positions are being filled. Then, I found myself putting in countless days of lifting and running in preparation for playing healthy junior year.

I did stay healthy that season and caught a touchdown pass. That spring, I was also able to travel to Florida with the baseball team in my first stint as student coach. As a physically healthy junior in college, that was a terrific spring break. Wearing sunglasses was often an absolute necessity as the weather was fantastic, and the beaches were sublime.

After that quality year and all the anticipation and excitement that had built up for my senior football season, all I got was one game. I made a block that was early in the first game of the year. While I made the down block correctly, it also sealed my fate resulting in a season ending shoulder injury. From highs junior year to now this, suddenly I couldn't help but feel like things weren't going my way. This was the last chance of my life to play football or any organized sport. All I could do was to play catch with one arm on the sideline, watching the last opportunity pass me by.

It was my senior year at Bluffton, and schoolwork was really becoming a pain. My love life was nonexistent then with another relationship ending less than a year before so there was no lady to give me comfort. To add to all that, my fun college life was nearing the end, so in my inexperienced view it was a rough period. Those emotions of despair and feeling sorry for myself put me in a funk. I made the choice that all my options were completely gone with nowhere to turn for solace. "Boxed wine Wednesdays" became a reality during football season senior year.

Please know, what had happened at that time with the shoulder injury and other college things was not as dark and dismal as it may sound. Deep down I knew it was time to look forward to the rest of my life. Most of my high school curriculum, including the community college courses I took while in high school, and all my schooling at Bluffton University had led me to the position I was in just before we left on the trip to Florida, and ultimately the accident.

I had grand plans of having a stellar nursing career, meeting the woman of my dreams, and raising a family in a great neighborhood not totally unlike the one I was raised in. Of course, I wasn't thinking much about children yet, but I was naturally assuming they would be somewhere in my future. By the grace of God, I was preparing to live a quality life.

Some people ask me where God was when all this happened. "It appears he left you and your group," they say.

I agree that it could in fact seem that way, but looking back on it, I see God everywhere.

In a journey of over 1,100 miles, the accident took place in a fifty-mile radius that allowed paramedics to arrive at the scene in minutes and get me to one of the best trauma hospitals in the nation so they could remove my spleen, or I would have bled out.

The accident occurred at a perfect time of day when there was basically no traffic in downtown Atlanta, Georgia. Being at that location also meant that one of, if not the best trauma hospitals in the entire country was located right off the freeway.

At the time of the accident, in the pre-dawn hours, not only was there no traffic, but the hospital was also in the middle of a shift change, providing them with double the staff for the emergency. If I had worked and planned for over fifty years, I could never have planned that kind of synchronicity. I know there was a bigger Author at work here.

That does not answer the question of why young, promising lives had to end or be forever altered that day. I have no idea why. The Lord works in mysterious ways, and I don't always understand or like it. But I choose to trust, as challenging and testing as that may sometimes be.

3RD INNING

Top of the 3rd
The Home Team
March-April 2007

Back home on the morning of March 2nd, Dad was watching the news before leaving for work at the United States Post Office in Monroe. It was just after six in the morning, and he was about to step out the door when he saw a breaking news alert on television, regarding a bus accident in Atlanta, Georgia. He thought, *With the time they left, that's about where they would be, but what are the odds of it being Bluffton? There's got to be hundreds of baseball teams going down to sunny Florida this time of year.*

After waking up to get ready for school, my sister, Tonya, opened her bedroom door to screaming. The news had reported that it was Bluffton University's bus that crashed.

Mom had come out to join Dad in the family room. They desperately began calling my cell phone. While anxiously watching the news footage of the accident, there was a point where Mom thought she saw me standing on the freeway. After another view of that same scene, she decided that it was not me, and so they were back to square one. Thus began the mountains of phone calls while trying to get information—any information—about their son. Not knowing initially if I was alive or dead, they pressed on.

My other sister, Trisha, then a nursing student at Lourdes University, told me later she heard the commotion while lying in bed and thought, *If it's a fire, they'll come and get me.* Such is the life of a nursing major. Mountains of reading and assignments meant that often it was fantastic to have a break and not worry or think about anything. She was entirely in that mode when all chaos broke loose.

After numerous attempts at calling my cell with no answer, and realizing the gravity of the situation, Mom and Dad were on the phone constantly trying to get information. They called my roommate at Bluffton, Josh Green. He was still asleep and had not heard anything about the crash, but said he'd check if anyone was available on campus who could give him information. Of course, the campus wasn't even awake yet, and nobody had arrived for the day that early, so that potential avenue of information proved fruitless.

Mom then called her adult niece and nephew who lived in Atlanta. Each cousin was about thirteen years my senior. One cousin explained to my mother that if she could tell him what hospital I was in, he would be able to tell her if my injuries were severe or not. The different hospitals in the area were known for their trauma levels and locals knew which hospital took and treated the worst injured trauma patients.

At this point, Mom knew nothing whatsoever, so he went to each hospital to try and find out if I was there, and injured, or if I had been killed.

As it turned out, all that cousin could find out was that I was in Grady Memorial Hospital, where EMTs had taken the most critically injured. In those tense moments, somehow my parents were informed that I "had a procedure done." It was not clear to them what that "procedure" was.

Finally, a doctor from Grady spoke to Mom on the phone and told her about my life-threatening injuries and my current critical status. Another baseball team member, Zach Arend also landed on the freeway. We each had similar injuries and it was difficult to tell us apart right then due to our similar body structures and massive amounts of head trauma.

Trisha had gone to get Tonya from school. To Trisha, the six-minute drive from our house to the high school felt like sixty. Walking from the parking lot to the high school office felt as if she were walking the distance of a marathon, as her mind was going a million miles an hour in a thousand different directions.

By now, the accident had become national news. Trisha entered the high school office and, after taking one look at her, the secretaries knew why she was there and paged Tonya down to the office for her excusal. My mother had instructed Trisha not to tell Tonya about my injuries until they got home so that everything could be discussed as a family but, as they began the journey home, Tonya kept insisting and begging to be filled in. Trisha was not even able to make it out of the school parking lot before spilling out to her what they thought were my injuries.

Tonya soon began to feel sick to her stomach, as she could feel the raw fear and emotion in Trisha's voice that told her things weren't looking good.

After they arrived home and the situation was fully explained, Tonya recalls Mom telling her, "You know how I usually tell you that it's not time to worry yet? Right now, it's time to worry."

As it turned out, at that time Grady Memorial was mixed up and the Berta family was being told of the injuries Zach Arend had instead of my own.

Back in Atlanta, Mom's niece was standing in Grady, and before her lay a surviving severely injured player so badly disfigured that she could not differentiate whether the individual before her was me. She called my mother to double check the color of my eyes. My cousin was told I had blue eyes. She looked at the injured player before her and lifted his eyelids. She saw he had brown eyes. In that instant, my cousin thought I was one of the players killed.

She weakly asked if there were any other unidentified surviving players. The staff told her there was one more and proceeded to lead her to a different room.

After lifting this boy's eyelids, she saw that this individual had blue eyes. Due to the severe injuries and massive swelling of the head she was still unsure if it was me. My cousin stood on a stool to get a better look and, looking down at the body, saw muscular shoulders. She remembered those shoulders from volleyball games at family reunions and at that point knew it was her cousin, Tim. She informed the staff who I was but knew nothing about the brown-eyed baseball player—not even his name. The Grady hospital did not know much more either. Later, it was confirmed the other player was Zach Arend.

Since Trisha had college and Tonya had high school to attend, at first only Mom and Dad left for the accident scene. After much chaos and hurried packing, Mom took a moment to compose herself and ask for God's help. Over my bed in my room was a cross with the "Footprints" poem on it.

Mom knelt on my bed and, placing her hand on that cross, asked, "For my son's life, that he might do your work, Lord." She had no idea just how close to death her son was.

Mom and Dad were driven to the Detroit airport by relatives who also lived in Ida. Come to find out, one airline had offered free flights to the families of the Bluffton University baseball team. That afternoon, my parents got on a plane to Georgia, not knowing their son's true condition, or even if he would still be alive once they got there.

After they arrived in Atlanta, they had to wait in line with the other victims' families to be debriefed. In addition to the debriefing, each family was assigned an individual who would help them through the process of getting information and finally connecting with their injured loved ones.

One Atlanta police chaplain was assigned to my parents. While standing in line for debriefing, with her head bent low and to the floor, Mom murmured, "I just want to see my son."

Though she had spoken in a soft whisper, that Chaplin heard her. "And you will," he said, leading them out of the line. He drove Mom and Dad to Grady Memorial Hospital.

When Mom and Dad arrived, they were taken to a room they thought was mine, but a staff member was standing guard outside the closed door. He would not let them enter no matter what Dad said to try and convince him. The pastor got in the young man's face trying to tell the guard who these people were, but to no avail. It was after eight p.m., and rules were in place due to the gang violence they often experienced around Grady Memorial. My parents had made this long journey from day to night, were standing outside my room and could not get in to see me.

Mom called her niece who had already been there and was in the hospital waiting room. She had been in the hospital all day, alternating her time between Zach and me, reassuring us our parents were on the way, even if we were unconscious and she had no way of knowing if we could hear her. Once she came and found my parents, she said, "Oh, that's Zach's room —Tim's over here."

After they were shown to my room and had stepped inside, even though they had just been told it was their son, the mutilated figure in front of them had no resemblance to who they knew it to be. Dad suddenly had to actively search for air because it took his breath away. Mom moved quietly to my bed and bent low to my unresponsive and unconscious body. She whispered, "Tim, Mom and Dad are here. We love you."

At that point my chest heaved, my vitals began to go through the roof, and I became extremely agitated. Well, as agitated as you could be when lying unconscious in a hospital bed after being thrown out of a bus as it went flying off an overpass.

A nurse nearby said to Mom, "Stand back—that's too much stimulation for him."

Backing up, Mom thought to herself, *Oh my God, he survives being thrown off an overpass—I've come all this way and now I've killed him!*

My primary injuries were numerous and substantial. My left lung collapsed and had to be reinflated. My spleen had already been removed. I've read and heard conflicting reports regarding the condition my ribs were in, so I'll just say all the ribs in my body were broken or at least cracked, and those on the left especially. My left collar bone was broken, along with my left shoulder blade.

Surgeons had removed a piece of my skull to give my brain room to swell. The doctors told my parents I had numerous bleeds on my brain and described my brain as being "red and angry." When they asked the doctors where my brain injury bleeds were located, my parents were informed, "All over."

When Mom and Dad inquired how many bleeds, doctors responded, "Too many to count."

Not exactly a positive or bright outlook.

———

In the early morning hours, a week after the accident almost to the minute, the tragedy claimed another victim. Zach Arend

43

passed away when his kidneys simply couldn't function any longer.

He and I had been running a fever. When the doctor came out of Zach's room pulling off his gloves, he kneeled and spoke directly to Zach's mom who was sitting on the floor and said, "We did all we could."

Mom and Dad have told me, even though they never met them before, they formed a significant bond with the Arend family during that time. The families had much in common, including small town rural life, athletic sons they were proud of, and a love of baseball. Both had younger daughters back at home and both possessed a deep faith in God.

Their sons, from the start, were the two most critically injured survivors and were being treated in the same hospital, only a short distance apart from each other. For each set of parents, it was their firstborn and only son that had sustained extreme and life-threatening injuries. The Berta and the Arend family's each had hopes and dreams and all talked of walking out of Grady hospital with their sons. Though both Zach and I were unconscious, our parents frequently talked to us out loud. They believed that we could hear them, somehow, and the hope was that their words would give us strength to pull through.

Shortly after Zach's death, Zach's father asked permission to go into my room and talk to me. Dad gave his consent, and Zach's father came into my room and gave me a pep talk. Standing over me, with a soft yet powerful voice, he spoke to me, "We have to have something good come out of this."

He said things other than that one sentence and of course this moment was described to me much later when I was conscious again, but I can only assume I heard him, since I had reacted so strongly to my mother's voice. His gesture is the definition of inconceivable courage.

During those first days in Atlanta, Karen had been praying for clergy to come in and visit. Yes, she probably could have called someone, but she was not exactly thinking clearly at this time. Her priority was to stay by my side through every moment and she was focused on that task.

After a few days, in came Father Kevin. Father Kevin was a priest who hailed from the same high school as a fellow baseball team member who had come to Bluffton from Georgia and had been on the bus. That player's injuries had been minimal enough that he was able to return to Bluffton shortly after the accident.

Whenever Father Kevin would come, he would talk to me out loud, calling me "Timbo." Every time he spoke to me, even if my vitals were way off, they would go back to normal. He also would appear at random-but-perfect times. On the nights I was restless, he would show up, and peace would come over me. When Zach died so exceedingly early that morning, the Reverend was there.

After Zach died, my father became very upset. He started to pace up and down the hallway outside my room. Both Zach and I had been running a fever, so Dad assumed I was next to die.

Father Kevin was walking down that hallway and saw how upset my dad was. He grabbed Dad and pulled him close to say something to him. Because of how agitated my father was, he was not able to make out what the clergyman said at first, but the priest waited for Rob to compose himself. Father Kevin then explained that now was not the time to feel guilty, that this event and its aftermath was out of everyone's control.

"There is something bigger at work here", the priest said.

My dad needed those simple words more than he knew. When Dad reflects on that day, he admits he did feel tremendous guilt. The guilt of his son living and Zach dying, even though he had no control or choice in the matter.

While part of my family was down in Atlanta, the Ida community was hard at work planning a fundraiser for the

Berta family. I had, unbeknownst to me as I lay unconscious, a "home team" rooting for me.

St. Joseph Church had—and has to this day—a banquet hall right across the street from the church. Grandma Berta and an aunt had volunteered to stay at our home with my younger sisters while Mom and Dad were gone. That aunt reported to my parents that the fundraiser had a line from the church hall to Lewis Avenue, the main street running through Ida.

I learned much later that this fundraiser did more than raise funds—the event itself, and Lourdes's participation in it, was the catalyst for my future. Since I had planned to become a nurse, using my biology degree from Bluffton as the starting point, I had applied to different nursing schools before the baseball team left Ohio for Florida. The letter of acceptance to Lourdes University had arrived at my home in the days just following the accident. My aunt received it in the mail after Mom and Dad left for Atlanta. She called and read them the news. As she read the acceptance letter, Rob and Karen cried.

Come to find out, when the administrators of Lourdes University learned of the accident, the president at the time, as well as the Board of Trustees, wanted to do something to help. When they became aware I had already been accepted, that "something" was to award me the first full-ride scholarship in the history of the school.

A representative from Lourdes stood up at the fundraiser and announced, "We do not know if Tim will ever be able to come back to school, but if he does, for anything he can do and as long as it takes him, he will not pay tuition at Lourdes University." Lourdes really stepped up to the plate and knocked it out of the park.

———

Bottom of the 3rd
Personal Reflections

I cannot imagine what it feels like to find out your child has been involved in a terrible accident hundreds of miles away.

The desperation and helplessness my parents must have felt when they heard the news, and when I repeatedly did not answer my cell phone, I cannot even fathom. I hope they truly know how grateful to God I am for having them as parents. I am appreciative for how my whole family handled my accident and recovery.

I am grateful for how true friends handled it as well. I am also thankful for the love and genuine caring of complete strangers through this whole ordeal. Looking back on all the get-well cards, the kind words and gestures, the mountains of prayers said for me, and the charitable events held on my behalf is humbling.

It was a true blessing extended family was so close and could help Mom and Dad pack and drive them to the airport. Upon arriving in Atlanta, another blessing was having cousins who lived there. Both willingly set aside their days and busy schedules to help my parents during a challenging and grim time in their lives. I am forever grateful, and I want them to know that.

Thinking back on that time—despite my lack of memory of it—makes me immeasurably sad at what I and others experienced, but at the same time, also enormously appreciative. My injuries could have been so much uglier, and even terminal, or I could have been without the support of family and expert medical providers. Why my injuries were not any worse, I'll never know, especially after being thrown out of a bus traveling freeway speed flying off an overpass.

Years later, while visiting a nursing class and discussing my injuries, I learned this: you can walk up behind somebody in the street and hit them as hard as you can with a hammer in the shoulder blade and you cannot break that bone. When I visit different nursing classes, I sometimes tell the nursing students that I forgot to bring a hammer so I could try to break the shoulder blade of a volunteer and prove my point. I have not yet had anybody volunteer.

The fact that the impact was so intense that I broke my shoulder blade, the second strongest bone in the body, makes me appreciate and realize how blessed I am to even function day to day. Of course, that functioning is limited and damaged —I used to be a great athlete but now I can barely use my left arm or hand. At times, I have trouble using my left leg, pushing off or walking, let alone much else athletic-wise.

Regardless of my limitations, I praise the Lord for the fact that I am still here and especially for the fortune of having been transported in a matter of minutes to one of the top trauma hospitals in the U.S.—or maybe even the world. That was a remarkable unexpected benefit in what was otherwise a dreadful experience. And to say "dreadful" doesn't even come close, to expressing the feelings for lives lost and for their families and friends left behind to grieve.

It is every coach's worst nightmare to lose a player, let alone five. I have a lot of respect for Coach Grandey. He is a good friend. I do not know how he was able to keep his sanity after the accident, but somehow, he did. Coach Grandey stayed inside the bus as it shot over the guardrail and was trapped between the front stair wall and the seat. His head was continually bashed back and forth, and he broke every bone in his face while also sustaining a concussion. He was in a face and neck brace for many weeks afterward.

Months after the accident, I saw him still in his neck brace, yet he was using a push mower to mow the baseball field (now Memorial Field) at Bluffton University. He strikes me as a guy who doesn't want you to feel bad for him—he's got too much work to do to lay around feeling sorry for himself. This is often the case in those who have been or are involved in sports, especially college athletics. They are accustomed to constantly being busy and productive. Coach Grandey's determination and motivation continues to be a source of inspiration for me, as does his bravery during that time. It turned out to be his turn at bat in a nearly impossible situation, but he came through in the clutch.

With lots of family help and support, Karen and Rob came through in the clutch as well. The support the Arend family gave my parents will never be forgotten, nor will the great pain Zach's mother and father must have felt when leaving the hospital without their son. The fact that Zach's dad found it in himself to come into my room shortly after his son had died shows me that he is a man of truly unimaginable valor and generosity.

Looking back, I realize what an incredible thing that was for Mr. Arend to do. To push aside the horror of that day for even a few minutes to come and encourage me, to have the determination to find some kind of light or redeeming factor in what was the worst possible tragedy a parent can face, tells me the kind of man Zach would have become had he lived. I am forever humbled and grateful for that gesture.

After being told of Mr. Arend's actions that day, I have since then only hoped that I can make him proud of what my life is now. I hope he knows I strive and fight for all my teammates who were killed, that I am trying to bring a light to the world and make something positive come of this terrible accident.

Speaking of positive, it is said it takes a village to raise a child. In addition to Coach Grandey, the Ida village stepped up to the plate and came through. The response of the entire Ida community is indescribable. To think an entire town stood behind somebody who graduated from high school there years before is inspiring. I credit my parents and the kind of people they are for part of the response from the town. They are people who too would have supported anyone in the Ida community if this accident had happened to someone else. As part of the Ida Village, I had something to do with that positive response as well and am grateful us Berta's all grew up there.

Speaking of siblings, it's tough to put myself in the shoes of Tonya or Trisha. I cannot imagine waking up to get ready for school and, instead, opening your bedroom door to screaming, and then the awful news that there is a very distinct possibility that your brother is dead. It's also hard to think of having one of your few times of rest while in nursing school be so rudely interrupted by such traumatic news.

Through high school and most of college, all I had to worry about were grades, athletics, and girls, not necessarily in that order. I certainly did not have to worry about any family member suddenly being in critical condition hundreds of miles away or being thrust into the spotlight of public news, but they did. Both Tonya and Trisha got conflicting information regarding the accident.

Tonya told me a high school classmate informed her the day of the accident that I was up and eating breakfast in Atlanta. Obviously not even close to the truth. Trisha kept getting conflicting reports from news accounts because no one knew any exact details.

Also, since the accident was big news at the time, both Tonya and Trisha were often pestered by national media. On tv during one story, Trisha saw footage of the four of them embracing and crying after Trisha had brought Tonya home from school the morning of the accident. The national media, unbeknownst to my family, had entered our home and recorded this deeply intimate moment. Later, Trisha told me she felt like a pawn used by national news to sell a story, with no regard for her feelings or the trauma she had experienced. That had to be challenging and I commend them both for how they dealt with the intrusions. I do not know how I would have handled all of that had I been in their place. All the events we remember having with local media and ESPN were positive experiences.

Mom and Dad were constantly praying, pleading, and imploring God to save my life and in their many prayers, were not afraid to let God know how frightened they were. "Lord, this is too big for us and it's just too much," they prayed. "We ask you to take the reins; we want to give this to you. Please help us figure this out because we are overwhelmed."

At some point following the accident, I also learned churches all over the U.S. and the world were praying for the Bluffton bus accident victims. I credit Mom and Dad immensely for this universal outpouring of love and support. And it is those many prayers, by family and strangers alike, that saved my life and got us through.

4TH INNING

Top of the 4th
Atlanta
March - April 2007

On day one of my hospital stay in Atlanta, doctors explained that the first twenty-four hours after the accident were the most critical. Mom and Dad did not want to leave the hospital during that time. Mom sat by my bedside and unceasingly prayed. Dad went to a visitors' waiting area and tried to sleep. At about 4 a.m., he came back to relieve Mom, who went to the waiting room area.

There were many others in that waiting room area who were there for different reasons and not associated with the Bluffton accident. There was a light permanently on by the restroom door—a door that did not shut properly and loudly banged with each opening and closing. Mom drifted back and forth from strange dreams to waking.

"Excuse me. Excuse me," a voice repeated. Mom thought she was dreaming, but the voice persisted. She struggled to open her eyes. There stood a tall gentleman with white hair. He was holding bags in each hand. "Excuse me, are you with the Bluffton baseball team?"

"Yes," Mom stammered as if just awakened while she struggled to take everything in.

In a low and gentle southern drawl, he said, "I brought these for you all."

Mom blinked.

"Donuts," he said. "Krispy Kreme donuts."

Mom knew nothing about Krispy Kreme donuts, but she knew kindness. She led him back to Dad, where the nurses showed them to a large room with tables and chairs where food was brought to feed large groups. Support from the community was immediately evident, and this gentleman wouldn't be the last individual to come offering sustenance.

When I survived the first twenty-four hours, my parents were elated, but were then told, "Really, the first forty-eight hours are the most critical." When I survived the first forty-eight hours, Mom and Dad were ecstatic, but then they were told, "It's actually seventy-two hours that are the most critical."

When I survived seventy-two hours Mom and Dad breathed a sigh of relief—I had made it.

The doctors then sat down with my parents and explained there were many hurdles ahead and stated, "One of the biggest hurdles is infection. It is not a matter of *if*, but *when* infection will set in, what will the infection be, and will he be able to survive it."

I was on a ventilator, had lost a lot of blood due to my ruptured spleen and abundant wounds, was in an induced coma, had had an emergency surgery to remove that spleen, and a separate emergency surgery to remove a piece of my skull. I was catheterized, IV-ed, and had a drainage tube in my head that allowed the blood and fluid in my skull to escape. The brain surgery incision was stapled but unhealed. There were numerous tubes and wires attached to me, and monitors that displayed glowing numbers of body stats splashing and changing endlessly. I lay in bed motionless and unresponsive. I'm not sure if I could have been more vulnerable to infection.

My sister, Trisha, the nurse, feels that, in hindsight, presenting my recovery in terms of a series of small goals was probably the best way to handle the situation when it came to my parents. The hospital staff breaking my chances of positive outcome down into clusters—twenty-four hours, forty-eight, and finally, seventy-two—made sense in terms of that. Grady Hospital did not just care about my own health and survival—they were concerned for my whole family and its emotional state.

My parents maintained an unwavering faith and a positive hopefulness. Despite their bright outlook, they still felt tremendous fear, and it was far better to digest the situation through the perception of little goals. Otherwise, the magnitude of my whole journey—the timeline, and a complete understanding of the size of the mountain they had to climb—may have crushed everyone's spirits.

———

Gradually, the surviving Bluffton baseball boys were cleared to return home. When it became apparent this would be a long haul for us Bertas, the nursing crew made a small vacant conference room available for the family to use. It was on my floor and had chairs lined up against the walls. Best of all, it was private and required a code to unlock the door. There, family members could take breaks, talk, eat, and even lie down on the floor to rest without leaving the hospital.

One nurse even offered to take Mom and Dad's clothes back to her home to do their laundry. They thanked her for her incredibly kind offer, but they declined. Mom tells me she thought, *Some stranger shouldn't have to wash our dirty clothes.* My parents and family would have been shocked then, if they had known just how long this journey was to be.

Our Krispy Kreme donut man continued to come and offer help. He really meant what he said, too. He offered Mom and Dad an extra car to use, a laptop, and brought them frequent hot meals from high-class establishments. He took Mom shopping for Easter so she would be able to give my sister, Tonya, an Easter basket when she was down in Atlanta over Ida High School's Spring break. To this day, Tonya has kept that Easter basket.

John the Krispy Kreme man would just sit with Rob and Karen at times, quiet if they were quiet, talked if they talked. He was not looking to get anything in return. He was just there for them for whatever they needed. A steady, caring presence.

There were more good people than him, too.

The first time Tonya flew back home from Atlanta to go back to school, she knew that there was a very good chance she could have seen me alive for the last time, and she was visibly shaken. A lady on the plane saw she was upset and thought she was just afraid of flying, so she held her hand. Tonya didn't bother to correct her, just felt comfort from this concerned stranger.

A local youth organization, the Buckhead Baseball Group, wanted to do something as well to help my family. My parents politely declined. One day a woman from Buckhead Baseball saw my dad resting on the floor of our make-shift family room through a thin window to the room.

"I need a list of what you need," she explained.

My dad thanked her but said, "We don't need anything."

She was insistent. "Now, you listen to me—I have thirty mothers lined up, desperately begging for some way to help. You are baseball, we are baseball, so why don't you let them help you out or bring some food or something?"

Dad groggily stated, "We could use some water."

After that, the flood gates opened. Buckhead baseball group members brought gallons worth of water and jugs of sweet tea. They brought food, an air mattress, pillows, and sheets. Soon my family had so much food coming at them all the time from Buckhead and the Krispy Kreme man that they would leave heaps of leftovers for Grady Memorial nurses in their break room.

A sidenote involving a nurse that herself was from Buckhead. There was a moment where my mom was found standing at my bedside in a puddle of my blood. Apparently, one of my blood tubes had popped, and mom hadn't noticed. This nurse calmly said, "I don't want to alarm you but you're standing in your son's blood." Mom recalls immediately feeling panicked but, on the outside, she remained calm for the nurse and stepped aside. The nurse simply cleaned up the mess and re-attached the tube.

When the day finally came of me being the sole survivor still hospitalized, it became glaringly obvious that my recovery was nowhere near complete. That had to be a difficult feeling for Rob and Karen. Despite all this support from locals, they were alone in their struggle.

As time wore on, family, friends, and local folks continued to be good to us. Certain staff members at the hospital went out of their way to show their kindness.

I had a nurse named James who was an incredible caretaker. He would even come in on his days off and shine a light in my eyes to check my brain activity. My parents would sometimes see him cleaning my room while speaking to me in his melodic Jamaican accent. He didn't go the extra mile for more money or recognition—he did it because he knew it would give me the best chance of survival.

As a nurse, James knew what the doctors had told my parents after they first arrived. He tried his hardest to minimize the impact of possible infections. As the days and weeks marched on, this thoughtful nurse continued to clean my room faithfully.

Despite everybody's best efforts, soon I began to run a fever. My family and friends who were present down in Grady Memorial ran a forehead-wiping brigade. They would stand in a line and would pass a wet cloth down to wipe my forehead. One person stood at the sink wetting a washcloth with cool water. After the rag was good and wet, they would pass it down the line for someone else to wipe my forehead. As soon as that wet cloth was used up and warm, it would be passed back down the line, and at the same time, another wet cloth that had been prepared was on its way to the front.

I'm also told that when my college and high school friends who had traveled down had to leave Atlanta to get back to their lives, they didn't want to leave.

Dad told them to go. "Tim would want you to go finish and build your life into your own dream. Go finish your education, build a good life, get married, have children. Live life for him, that's what he would want you to do."

———

Twenty-five days after the March 2nd accident, it looked as though it might be game over.

As it turned out, the fever I was running was from pseudomonas, a bacterial form of pneumonia. It was close to the scheduled time for me to leave Atlanta and be moved elsewhere for further rehabilitation. When the medical professionals discovered what was causing my fever, the leave date was postponed, and doctors gave my parents two options to get rid of it: antibiotics or surgery. There was a possibility I could die if they chose the surgery route. Without a doubt, they chose antibiotics.

That same evening, doctors took another look at the infection and told Mom and Dad, "It's worse than we thought. The antibiotics are not having any impact and are not going to save Tim. There is a good chance he may die during the operation, but if we don't do surgery the pseudomonas will kill him anyway."

My dad signed a paper stating the possible outcome of my surgery was death, but he knew it was my only chance. The odds of surviving a pseudomonas infection for anybody is poor, and regardless of previous health, roughly half of the people who get pseudomonas will die. I can't imagine what my odds were since I was already in such a compromised state.

Since the infection was much worse than originally thought, the surgery took longer than they told Mom and Dad. What was supposed to be a four-hour surgery turned into roughly an eight-hour operation as the surgeons fought once more to save my life.

To operate, the surgeon was sitting at a computer screen. He would be driving a device like a remote-controlled car and would use it to snip and peel off small sections of the film the bacteria were growing and wrapping around my lungs. The film would unavoidably rip as the device peeled strips of it off my lungs. There was also an abscess on the lower piece of one of my lungs. A small piece in that lung had to be completely cut off and removed.

Mom, Dad, and John spent what felt like an eternity waiting in their makeshift family room restlessly, presuming that at any moment they would finally be updated on how the surgery was progressing. When the operation went beyond four hours, Dad told me he thought for sure I was dead. Each time the hallway door opened Mom thought, *It's the doctor coming to tell us Tim has died.*

A fifth hour passed and, into the sixth hour, my grandma,

my mom's mother, called to check. Mom poured out to her in anguish.

"Mom, I'm so scared," she said.

In a strong, firm voice, my grandma replied, "Karen, have faith."

Renewed hope and deep breaths filled my mom. Sometimes you just need some encouragement. Hours after that phone call the hospital staff finally emerged down the hallway, pushing me on the gurney. Mom and Dad were elated and relieved. Come to find out, the hospital had tried to update them but the staff member the hospital had sent couldn't find them.

With the infection ravaging my body, I had not moved much. Now that it was gone, Karen and Rob were ecstatic to see I was flailing my arms and very much alive as I was being rolled down the hallway.

———

Two nights after the surgery, my aunt, Jane, had been the family member who volunteered to stay the evening with me.

The next afternoon was the new opening day for Bluffton baseball. The players on the team who had minor bumps and bruises were somehow able to muster enough courage to continue the season. Today, I think back and commend them. You have seen and suffered things nobody should have to see or experience, especially at such a young age. Well done, teammates!

Aunt Jane was reading aloud sports articles to me along with perhaps informing me that Bluffton's opening game was that day. She thought that, even though I was unresponsive, there was a chance I might be listening.

On one occasion, she looked up to check on me and thought she saw my eyes flutter. She blinked, looked again but still wasn't sure. She stood up to get a better look. Sure enough, my eyes were half open!

She ran to the doorway, yelling, "Come! Help! He's opening his eyes!"

Medical staff swarmed the room. When they saw my eyes were open, the staff surrounded my bed and wildly began talking.

My nurse, James, was there and knew this was an opportunity he could not let pass. He started to shout, "Tell him to do something, tell him to do something!"

The medical staff around me began to give me instructions all at once, but soon another thought occurred to James.

"Wait! He doesn't know anyone here, but he knows you," he said, enthusiastically pointing to Aunt Jane. He rushed around the side of the bed, grabbed her, and dragged her over in front of me shouting, "He knows you—tell him to do something!"

Aunt Jane, entirely flabbergasted by all the ensuing chaos, leaned down beside my bed and asked, "Tim, can you raise a finger?"

After I raised my right pointer finger, James became even more excited. He grabbed Aunt Jane by the shoulders while shaking her and joyously yelling, "Do you know how huge that is?"

She had no idea what to say—she was too stunned. Yes, the first time I opened my eyes since the accident coincidently occurred on Bluffton's new opening day, March 30th. That day marked just one of many occasions that would give my family the hope and determination to move forward.

———

After my lung surgery, one of the greatest home run hitters in the history of baseball, the late Hank Aaron—Hammerin'

Hank, as he was known—came to the hospital unannounced to visit, one baseball guy to another. It was now almost two weeks into April, well over a month since I had first been admitted.

After he gowned up and put on gloves to go into my room, he simply sat by my bedside and talked to me. After he walked into my room, Mom was there and was in disbelief, asking him if he had the wrong room. After stating he was here to see Tim Berta, my mom told my sister, "Tonya, go get Dad."

Dad was in our makeshift family room. Tonya went to find my father and said to him, "Dad, Mom wants you to come down to Tim's room—some big baseball guy is there."

Hank Aaron is one of the greatest players to ever play the game, so yes, I'd have to agree that his visit was an enormous deal. However, on that day, one of the best baseball players in the history of the game was just a regular guy chatting with my parents. In fact, according to him, it was much easier to hit baseballs than to sell cars. He talked about his family—his mother in particular—and said he'd rode a lot of buses in his day.

Mom kept imploring me to wake up. "Son, wake up. Tim, it's Hank Aaron. *Hank Aaron*. Please, wake up. Can you open your eyes? Oh, Tim, you are never gonna believe this. You've got to wake up. You're gonna be so sad if you miss this. Tim?"

Nothing from me, not even a twitch. But through this entire exchange, Hank was smiling his easy smile, relaxed, comfortable, chuckling sometimes and talking to me as if I was awake. The Grady staff casually continued to walk by my door to get a glimpse of Hank Aaron.

When Hank Aaron arrived, he signed the lobby visitor book as required. Coincidentally, and about twenty minutes after he left, my uncle who was the sports editor for a newspaper, came in to visit. When he signed the visitor book, he looked at the name above his and had to read it a few different times because he didn't believe the name he saw. He was disheartened when he found out it was the real Hank Aaron and that he had just missed him.

———

James continued to be a caring staff member at Grady, and I will never forget the stories I have been told about him—he always wore different beanies while on duty to cover his dreadlocks. My parents had surprised him one day with a new Bluffton beanie. James was a man of action but very few words. The day that beanie was given to him, tears ran down his cheeks, touched deeply by their small act of kindness. Rob and Karen were all grins the day James wore that beanie for work.

My family soon learned the new day that was set for me to leave Atlanta and be flown up to another hospital in Toledo, Ohio. The evening before leaving, my family had begun to say goodbye and thank you to the hospital staff. It had been a month and a half since the accident. Most of the staff and people of Atlanta had been exceptionally kind and generous to them. Then it came time to say goodbye to James, who was at the hospital that night.

As James was hugging Dad goodbye, he said, "Don't worry, Poppi—he gonna be all right."

Dad said, "I hope you're right. Whenever we ask any other medical staff what kind of recovery we can expect, the only response we get is, 'We don't know. Brain injuries are impossible to predict.' So how do you know that?"

"He got lots of love and caring folk around him, and whenever I shine my light into his eyes, I can see him. He's in there."

Dad replied, "James, I hope you're right."

After spending six weeks at Grady Memorial Hospital and surviving my accident injuries, numerous subsequent surgeries, and the pseudomonas infection, I was finally released. I could not go home yet—that wouldn't be for a few more months—but I was able to be transferred to the University of Toledo Medical Center (UTMC) in Toledo, Ohio. Toledo would be much closer for my family to visit. Mom and Dad could also return to work.

The night before we were to fly home, from their hotel room, my family could see the sky lit up with fireworks from the Atlanta Braves Major League baseball stadium. I am sure to many it was just another fireworks show, but to the Berta family, it signaled an appropriate marker for this milestone in my recovery.

Since my parents had to go back to work and we had to make the journey back to my region, doctors in Atlanta researched where the best spot to send me for rehabilitation in the Southeast Michigan/Northwest Ohio area would be. They decided UTMC was a good fit, so I was flown there on a special medical flight. My mother had volunteered to be the family member who would fly with me. There were only five of us on the med flight: my mom, two nurses from Grady Memorial, the pilot, and me.

The two nurses were there in case something went wrong medically. Sure enough, during the medical flight to Toledo, something went wrong. Mom's best guess is that my blood pressure began to severely fluctuate, possibly due to the air cabin pressure changes. The flight nurses began to frantically perform procedures, and they yelled for Mom to give them a certain medical instrument.

There was a large bag of different medical devices next to

her, and looking into the bag, she did not know what anything was, let alone the one they needed. She knew whatever was wrong at the time sounded vital, but which piece of equipment? Finally, in a panic, Karen said a quick prayer for guidance, blindly reached in the bag, grabbed something, and thrust it toward them. As it turned out, the object she gave them was exactly the one they needed. My blood pressure stabilized and what could have been a major issue was not.

When we touched down in Toledo on the same day, April 14th, it was snowing. Like the fireworks, arriving in Toledo was certainly a milestone marker and the fact it was snowing may also have been a symbol.

Bottom of the 4th
Personal Reflections

Try to put yourself in this situation. You are hundreds of miles from home in a place you have never been, and your son is fighting for his life. You are scared to death and scared of death. At the same time, there are a multitude of people from various organizations, both medical and non-medical, wanting to make your stay as comfortable as possible, given the circumstances.

If I had been given the choice of selecting not only where the accident would take place, but what kind of people would seemingly come out of the woodwork, I am convinced—based on everything I have heard—that I could not have made a better choice.

The people in Atlanta showed us Bertas Southern hospitality from the goodness of their hearts, and I am forever grateful. I cannot say thank you enough for what the people of

Atlanta, our Krispy Kreme man, the Buckhead baseball group, Father Kevin, Hank Aaron, and my cousins did for my family while I was incapacitated.

Of course, it saddens me to think that I do not remember that good aspect of Atlanta. Though none of the kind buzz of activity around me registered, I saw afterward the way in which God was taking care of us and giving people in Atlanta the opportunity to provide for us.

To all the kind strangers who supported my family, and to the nurses and doctors in Grady Memorial Hospital in Atlanta, for their outstanding skill and care, to all my family and friends who journeyed down to Atlanta and helped in different ways, and even to the different spring sports teams who came to visit while passing through Atlanta also on their way to Florida, I want to say thank you. Thank you to my Bluffton roommate, who was in Atlanta the very next day.

Thank you to Father Kevin, for visiting and giving us peace.

Thank you to James, for coming in on your days off to check on me. Thank you for cleaning my room, even though that was not your job.

Thank you to the head nurse who offered to take my family's laundry back to her home and do laundry for them—she was also one of the two nurses who flew with me back to Toledo. Your kind offer to do my family's laundry is very much treasured. If it would make you feel better, you can do my laundry anytime you want—I'll let you. Though I joke, I do know for a fact, my family very much appreciated that kind gesture. That's another story I tell the nursing classes I visit; to show them how integral compassion is to the job. I also tell them if they would ever need some practice in doing laundry for patients, they can do mine.

Kind gestures and love came from extended family as well,

one being my aunt, Jane, who volunteered to stay the night in Grady. I don't blame her for being completely shocked when James, my nurse, was shaking her by the shoulders after I opened my eyes and followed her directions. As it turns out, that moment *was* huge because it meant my brain was still functioning. My brain could take in the request, process that request, and send the signal to my fingers to move, and my fingers could move. That simple act told James and the doctors a whole lot about my brain function at that moment. For that too, I am grateful.

I really wish my memory, or anything at all for that matter, had been functioning when Hank Aaron willingly came and sat down to talk to me. I never saw him play—I only saw small clips of his swing and know about his records. I will not talk about records or speak of how great a baseball player he was, because that goes without saying, but I will thank him for the good man he was. I want the world to know how much joy it brings me to tell people that one of the greatest home-run hitters of all time had a good enough heart to gown up, glove up, and come into the hospital for a young man about whom he knew nothing. My parents speak of how genuine a human being you were to us that day, and I cannot express enough how much your visit meant and still means to them. They needed all the levity and inspiration they could get during those days, and I get lots of joy from telling people I met Hank Aaron. I wish I could have talked with you and shaken your hand. To this day, I jokingly tell people I have met Hank Aaron, and at the same time tell them I have not met Hank Aaron, because I remember nothing of his visit. He was just able to arrive, too, because we were flying out of Atlanta shortly after that.

On the flight to Toledo, Mom selecting exactly the correct medical tool out of the bag is telling. That may sound like a spot of blind luck, but I choose to think that there was a bigger

Author orchestrating even this small task, and that Author had given my mother and me a victory.

Parents usually want what's best for their child and my parents were no exception. Upon arrival at UTMC, they wisely humbled themselves, realizing the medical staff and therapists were professionals whose job was to rehabilitate me in the best most effective way possible. In Rob and Karens' meeting with the therapy staff, they made their stance on this apparent. They expressed their desire to help, if possible, but helping was not a demand.

As plans for my rehabilitation and inpatient care were discussed, my parents said something along the lines of, "Look, we want you to get him as far back as you can. This is what you went to school for, this is your area of expertise. We don't know anything about rehab or medicine, so we want you to guide us and do your very best for our son. If you need us to help, we will do what we can and if you need us to get out of the way, then we will. Please just bring our son back."

That kind of confidence and faith is love in its truest form, and I am beyond grateful.

The fact that fireworks were going off the night before my family and I left Atlanta is very fitting. It was obviously a celebration for everyone, but for us personally it signified a major transition marking all the progress I had made. That is, until we touched down in Toledo, and it was snowing in April. When we took off from Atlanta the temperature was in the 70s—when we landed in Toledo it was in the low 40s. The nurses wrapped my whole body in foil because of the drastic temperature drop. Talk about a letdown—it almost makes me glad I was out of it at the time.

Thinking about it now, the fireworks in Atlanta and the spring snowfall in Toledo may have had a deeper meaning. Maybe God was speaking to us. Telling us that the milestone of survival and leaving Atlanta was worth a celebration with the fireworks. Perhaps the spring snow was a warning that, even though it may seem like spring, winter was hanging on and I still had a long tough recovery ahead.

But regardless of how long, harsh, and cold a winter is, God always ensures springtime arrives. And my springtime was coming.

5TH INNING

Top of the 5th
Holy Toledo!
April - June 2007

I slowly opened my eyes, taking in the room. I had no inkling of everything that had just taken place. Not a clue. Those first few seconds of waking up were like being in a fog—I didn't know what I had been doing, or where I was when I had gone to sleep. Because of this, there was no reason to think anything was out of the ordinary, and I naturally assumed those pieces of information would all come back instantaneously, as they always did when I woke. That moment stretched on, and I kept waiting for something, anything, to come, but nothing did.

My brain was void of memory.

As the seconds became minutes and still no memory came, I became anxious. The first thing I noticed was that I was lying in an uncomfortably firm bed, which felt foreign. I knew I wasn't in my bed at Bluffton.

My anxiety deepened as my eyes searched the room. From the time of the accident—a month and a half ago up until now

—I had not been aware of my thoughts or cognizant of anything going on. Or at least had not remembered if I was. Since I was now, I realized I was surrounded by machines flashing and beeping as if they were alive. Machines that seemed to shout at me—*HOSPITAL!*

My mind swirled with questions I had no answers to— *Where am I? Why am I here?* I knew *who* I was, and the last thing I could remember was being perfectly healthy—and certainly not being injured or sick to the point of needing a hospital. The last thing I remembered was… nothing.

The next thought flashing through my head was almost physically painful: *Is my family okay? Did whatever happen to me also happen to them… or worse?*

I searched the room again, frantically this time, hoping for any clues as to the welfare of my family. Across the room, my mother sat in a chair reading. Relief swept over me like a cool breeze in the outfield on a humid day. She didn't look too upset, so I assumed whatever had happened must not have been that terrible—and at least I knew she was alive. Of course, I had no idea the only reason she didn't look upset was because the terrible thing that had happened was something that, over the course of about two months, she had been forced to become accustomed to as her new reality.

Since I didn't know any differently, I considered just getting out of bed—I assumed I could.

I did not get out of bed. Even the thought of moving brought on complete fatigue, and I had no idea where that exhaustion came from. It was as if I had just played an entire football game and never left the field the whole game. I was entirely drained.

The problem was… I did not remember playing a football game, or any kind of game, just before waking up in this place. What *had* I been doing? More importantly, what had I been doing that landed me in a *hospital*? I was exceedingly curious about how exactly I got where I was and was still concerned about the welfare of the rest of my family.

I could feel everything and move my limbs but, because I lacked information, did not even give it a second thought about how lucky I was to be able to feel and move limbs considering what had happened to me, whatever that was.

I closed my eyes and tried to concentrate on remembering. Nothing came to me. Not a single scrap of memory. I tried even harder to wrack my brain, to come up with anything that would help me make sense of this. Nothing. I didn't remember going to bed in this place and I certainly didn't think I needed a hospital.

Confusion turned to panic, especially when I saw someone in scrubs whom I did not know come into the room and Mom, to my bewilderment, acted like she knew her. This 'scrubs lady' didn't come in with anything nurses usually have, so I was further confused. She was, however, wearing scrubs as hospital staff do, and was going over to a wheelchair I had not noticed earlier that sat off to the side.

Was there someone else in this room I hadn't seen who needed a wheelchair? Perhaps she was taking the chair somewhere else, to someone who needed it? I felt a small stab of pity as was the case whenever I saw a person in a wheelchair. I wondered what happened to this person and why they needed a wheelchair. The cool breeze of relief hit my face again. I was so glad I didn't need one of those things.

I realized the woman was wheeling the chair over to my bed. The cool breeze turned to suffocating humidity.

That's silly, I thought. *She must not know about me. I'm a good athlete, and I can walk, so she must not be coming for me with that thing.*

It soon became apparent she *was* in fact coming for me. As I watched her lock the wheels in place near the bed, my panic became anger, though, for whatever reason, the thought never entered my mind to use my voice and ask, "Hey, what's going on here?"

My mother didn't seem to have any objections, and it was as if she had been doing this routine her whole life. Emotions regarding this massive betrayal churned within me—disbelief, confusion, and rage all threatened to rise to the surface, but somehow, I remained silent.

Inside my head, I screamed, *I'll get out of bed. I'll show them how I can handle this—it's not like I haven't been walking ever since I can remember.* As I tried to get up, my legs would not do what I was telling them to do. I began to get more and more angry and started to yell at my legs in my mind.

Come on legs, move! I urged them, but nothing happened. I could feel the blankets on my legs and feel my legs, but they would not cooperate with what my brain was telling them.

As I attempted to sit up, a heaviness more intense than any weight-lifting exercise I had ever done overcame me. It was as if there was a lock on my left arm holding it in place across my chest. Both legs, my left arm, and my chest felt as though each had a thousand-pound weight strapped to them. This made every effort of movement, whether it was lifting my torso, swinging my legs across the bed, or even turning my head, a Herculean task that required my whole attention and effort.

During the struggle to move, the athlete inside emerged, urging me to prove myself. *Come on, you can do this. You've done things ten times harder than moving around while you are lying down. Being a capable healthy athlete has been a part of you your whole life, so just do it already!* As I inched toward the edge of the bed, the scrubs lady was on one side of me and my mother had come over to be on the opposite side and they both assisted in sliding me off the bed into the wheelchair.

I was taken aback at how little assistance I was able to give them. It seemed like my best was not good enough. Just then, an ugly uncomfortable bicycle-type helmet was strapped onto my head.

Now what the heck is this? I wondered. *Why do I need this stupid thing? What could possibly happen to me while in this stupid wheelchair that would merit the need of this stupid ugly helmet that's too tight on me anyway? What gives?*

As the scrubs lady began to wheel me out of the room, confusion and anger threatened to take over my very soul. Yet there was no way to express it.

My captor began to wheel the wheelchair into a larger white room with other people inside doing various activities, like walking between parallel bars or rotating bicycle pedals with their hands. Once we were inside, my mind began unfolding a flurry of questions that followed a pattern like this: *Why am I in this wheelchair and what is this place? Why is my left arm stiff? Why does it hurt to unclench my left fingers? Why does my left foot feel immovably locked, and why is it aching?*

Looking around, I reasoned, *The tasks in this place don't look too difficult. If all I must do in this room is wheel those bicycle pedals with my hands... I am so above that. Don't they know me—don't they know who I am? Don't they know I played college football? This should be a piece of cake. I'll make short work of this place and show them.*

The fact left me that I was in a wheelchair, and I focused instead on the fact that I had no clue where I was or why I was there. The thought never entered my mind to use my voice and ask questions, like why am I here, or what's going on? I could only think about one thing at a time.

I did not work bicycle pedals with my hands—or do anything remotely strenuous, like get on a treadmill or lift barbells. Instead, scrubs lady rolled me to a giant vertical peg board shaped like a plus sign. It looked like something young children would use in a preschool setting. Were these people for real?

Apparently, they were. A different woman at the board began telling me what to do. I'm sure she introduced herself or gave me some other greeting, but the root of what she was telling me to do left me puzzled and was all I could focus on.

"I would like you to take these pegs and plug them into these holes in the board in front of you using only your left hand."

I had already forgotten all my thoughts and the whole ordeal that had just taken place in my room and my brain had moved on to confusion and frustration about this pegboard. *Why is she having me put pegs on this board, especially with my left hand? My left hand is stiff and hard to move.*

Why it was stiff and tough to move never entered my mind. The thought crossing my mind was, *Doesn't she know I could do this much quicker and better with my right hand?*

I had always been a goal-oriented, striving type of person, and that aspect of my personality was still intact. I secretly hoped she would leave for a moment so I could use my right hand to get this board filled much faster.

On the rare occasion she turned away to do something else and wasn't looking, I would use my right hand and quickly jam as many pegs in the board as fast as I could. The question of why I was being made to do this task with my left hand never ran through my mind—I was merely angrily following instructions but thought I had a much better and smarter way of accomplishing this task.

After struggling for a while to fill spaces with tiny pegs using my left hand and occasionally sneaking some in with my right, I was rolled into another room. This room was much less spacious than the large white room and was made even more tiny by a small woman sitting behind a large desk. I had already forgotten about the peg board and the only thing in my head now was what the lady behind the desk was going to have me do.

What she did next was insulting to my intelligence. She instructed me to complete simple arithmetic problems she placed in front of me. The first problem was something effortless, like 3 + 1. Yet, it was anything but effortless.

It wasn't that I did not know the answers, but more that my brain was easily distracted and took longer to function. For example, I would look at an easy problem like 3 + 1 and, instead of writing down the answer right away and moving on, I would begin to think lots of different things.

I don't remember these thoughts word for word, but after she asked me if I had any questions, my thought process went something like this: *Any questions? These are simple, no-thinking-required math problems. I mean come on now. Don't you know that I was in college studying biology? I passed organic chemistry, physics, and calculus? Don't you know I played football and baseball at the collegiate level? Somebody should tell these people about me—I wonder who will tell them? These are basic, no-thinking-required addition problems. If anyone had a question regarding these problems, they would have serious issues!*

I do not remember this specific thought train either, but my thoughts would often continue like this after I started looking at the problems. *This is so simple—I wonder what grade I was in when I first learned this stuff? Was it kindergarten or first grade? If it was kindergarten, I wonder what the simple thing used to explain it was? Was it apples? If it was apples, did we get to eat them? I hope so. If we did get to eat them, did they wash them? If not, that's gross, but I was in kindergarten, so I probably didn't care. Washing them reminds me, I wonder where they got the apples? Did the classroom aide get them? Did we have an aide? I'm pretty sure we had one when I was in kindergarten, but I also went to pre-kindergarten, and did we have an aide then? I don't remember an aide in pre-kinder-garten. Anyway, when I was in kindergarten, what was that aide's name? Was it April, or am I just confusing that name with a character in a cartoon show I used to watch? What show was that again?*

Distracted thoughts would consume me and lead me off on one mental wild goose chase after another. After reading all of this, you might be thinking, "Sheesh, I'm exhausted! Why couldn't you just shut up and do the problem—it's not that hard!" I agree. Again, it's not hard, but this is where my brain was. Not only was I physically exhausted from the rehab exercises, but this mental chaos had me constantly drained.

After the simple problems were finally completed, or time in the session ran out, my mom backed me out of the tiny room in my wheelchair. I had forgotten until then that Mom had been with me earlier in the day.

Once we cleared the door frame of the room, we turned around, and I was suddenly in another large, darker room. Although this room was not as big as the room with the tread-mill and peg board I had been in earlier, there were other people in here eating, and it reminded me of a cafeteria. I had been in cafeterias my whole life, so I knew what goes on here! I forgot all about the insult to my intelligence and the tiny room and prepared to focus on one of my favorite tasks—eating.

Gosh, I was excited. All this confusion with strange people I didn't know, going to places I had never been, using a wheel-chair I thought I didn't need, putting pegs in a board for no good reason, all intermixed with regular bouts with anger, had worked up an appetite. As the heaviness of my body had hit me earlier, it abruptly felt as though I had not eaten in days. I wondered what they were going to give me to eat.

I do not remember how I got the plate; I just remember being happy I was finally going to eat some food. I looked down, curious to see what I'd been served and... Wait a minute.

What was all this gooey, soft stuff? What had been placed before me was decidedly *not* food. It was... I didn't even know what it was. It kind of resembled normal food, at least in color, but, upon further exploration with what passed for a fork in this place, I discovered that it was nothing solid, just all mush. Maybe some type of casserole sort of thing? I didn't know what it was, but I did know it was not very good.

It's a good thing I was not a picky eater—plus, I was extremely hungry. Everything that had just happened to me within the last couple hours may not sound like much, but I had worked up an appetite. It never even occurred to me to ask what was going on or to try using my voice at all. I was just famished.

In addition to the food tasting awful, eating itself was a chore. I could not coordinate myself to take a simple bite and each time I made up my mind to try harder, I ended up spilling the food all over myself.

At times, Mom and Dad, or a member of my extended family, would need to feed me. I was being spoon-fed food I was not crazy about, was being wheeled to places I had no desire to go, was doing all sorts of strange and seemingly pointless tasks I did not want to do—all the while not knowing why I was even doing them. Not only that, but I was being forced to wear a helmet that was hot, extremely uncomfortable, and was making me sweat bullets.

To top it all off, I could not get any restful sleep due to my vitals being checked every hour throughout the night. Each morning that I was forced to get out of bed was its own unique adventure, laden with challenges and pitfalls. The simple tasks I used to take for granted—like brushing my teeth, using the toilet, being forced to somehow consume this thing they called breakfast, or getting dressed—each presented their own distinctive struggles and trials. Talk about a miserable and angry time. That epoch of despair and desperation was one of the darkest periods of my life. I felt hopeless and defeated.

I didn't know much, but I did know I wanted to leave this place as quickly as I could. That is, until this moment. I do not recall what day or time of day it was, or the situation, but I do remember exactly how I felt. When she first walked into my room, it was as if I had never seen an attractive female before, and I could not take my eyes off her.

Whenever I would watch her, I would abruptly forget whatever I was annoyed or frustrated about and suddenly my new world had a piece of normal in it. Even the stale smell of the hospital instantly left. It felt like a breath of fresh air. Maybe this awful, miserable place was not so bad after all. I wasn't speaking yet, but I would often tell myself, *I hope she's here today and comes into my room.* Perhaps I could not remember much of anything else from that time, but the gorgeous young nurse was stuck in my head.

Unfortunately, her occasional presence wasn't a fix for the bigger issues I was experiencing. On top of everything happening to me, I felt "those people" were having fun at my expense. In my head, I referred to the therapists and hospital staff as "those people" because I did not know who they were, but because of all the torture they were putting me through, I assumed they did not like me, and I knew with no uncertainty that I did not like them.

At some point, I had convinced myself "those people" were just making me do things to get a laugh at my struggles and see how much torment I could take before I just up and quit. And that was not the worst part about the whole experience. The worst was yet to come.

———

Bottom of the 5th
Personal Reflections

Looking back now on that time in UTMC when I first became aware of my hospital room, I don't know if I really had just awakened from a sort of light sleep into full lucidity, or if that moment was simply the point when I could start to remember the things I remember now. Either way, I assume everybody knows what I mean when I describe that instant in the morning when you first wake up. It's less than a second that you don't know where you are. Thankfully, that momentary state of confusion often clears up immediately.

Now imagine how disturbing it was to have that bewildering sensation not go away. I kept telling myself that the dense fog I was in would go away, that my memory would all come back—that it *had* to come back—but it didn't. Not having any memory at all of anything significant or any period is worrisome in most scenarios, but especially when you suddenly realize you're in a hospital, and you have no vigor or strength left inside of you.

Complete and utter fatigue does not even begin to accurately represent or describe how it felt for me. There was nothing there. I mean *complete* emptiness. There was no energy, no motivation and nothing in my brain to tell me what had happened or what was going on. It seemed like there was nothing much happening in my brain, especially in terms of interest or enthusiasm, until presented with a simple $3 + 1$ arithmetic problem.

Thus began a long rabbit trail leading me far away from what I was supposed to be doing—or at least what "those people" thought I was supposed to be doing.

It was only later that I found out why I was being subjected to various menial tasks—nobody knew where the level of my brain activity was and what I could handle at that time. That's why they gave me simple arithmetic problems. My mom explained to me years afterwards that as she and the speech pathologist sat there and watched me stare at that 3 + 1 problem, Mom thought to herself, "Does he not grasp how to do this? Is he trying to remember? Oh my, this is going to be rough." Neither she nor the speech pathologist knew what was going on inside my brain. They had no way of recognizing I understood and knew the answer, but my focus and thoughts were miles away from those simple problems.

You might be telling yourself, "Well, if I was in his situation of not knowing what was going on, I would certainly not be so willing to just go along and not question those around me. I would definitely scream in frustration if I was not able to use words to get my uncertainty across."

I would agree with that sort of logic—anyone in their right mind should have been doing just that, but I was not in my right mind. As a result, of course I submitted to whatever it was I was asked to do with no will or energy to resist. I could only think to do one thing at a time, and my thoughts came to me at an incredibly slow pace.

The "thinking" of each day generally followed this pattern: once I had gotten over (or more accurately, forgotten) the aggravation and confusion of not knowing where I was and what was wrong with me, then I moved onto why the heck I needed to be using a wheelchair. I then forgot about that and moved onto trying to figure out what the new room I was being wheeled into was and who the new people in this room were, even though each room and the people were the same every day. I soon forgot and moved on to being angry at being hungry and couldn't wait to eat.

Then, when I went to eat, I became incensed and curious as to why eating was extraordinarily difficult and why the food was mushy and disgusting. The next thought was that I was annoyed and incredibly tired, and I couldn't wait to go to bed, and so on.

In my old life, there was a piece inside of me that I referred to as the "athlete in me." The "athlete in me" would say things like *keep going, don't be weak, don't let up, if you don't do it somebody else will, just push through,* and different motivators in self-talk. When those self-talk tools did not work, I became increasingly agitated and more and more angry. Those things had gotten me through bad, tough times before, but now they were letting me down. Something I had relied on consistently and used regularly as support throughout my entire life suddenly was not working. I didn't know the reason why my body was not functioning the way it had before, and as you can imagine, it was infuriating.

My extended family, especially my mom's uncle Troy and aunt Kay, who would come to visit frequently, would help my mom or dad to feed me. We were given bath towels for my bibs, easily using over 10 bath towels during each feeding. I felt like a baby. I honestly had no idea my food had to be puréed for my own safety—I just thought it stunk. Even though the hospital had to puree all my food, they still displayed it as if it were not blended up, adding insult to injury. They would form the blended-up food to resemble actual chicken, or actual green beans, or other solid foods. It was bad food in disguise.

Today, understanding why the food was the way it was, I appreciate their efforts to make terrible food look good. But, as grateful as I am, if I get to choose, I will never be on that specific diet again.

Sometimes I had other special things going on that would make me forget all about the food, like the lovely nurse.

The stunning nurse meant more to me than what she would mean to a typical college-aged guy. Yes, my physical attraction to her was certainly a big part of it, but she meant much more to me than that in the context of my long-term predicament.

In my new world of despair and confusion, she gave me hope. She embodied a tangible picture of what I had wanted for my future and where I thought my life was headed prior to the accident. I had intended to be a nurse anesthetist, and to raise a family with a successful, smart, gorgeous woman like her. That young nurse was a walking, talking, visible piece of the future I was certain I was going to have, a tangible element of the world "old Tim" had been so close to. In her, I saw what I had been planning on.

In this chaotic realm of disarray and anger, the young nurse and everything she symbolized brought me peace and happiness.

What did not bring me peace was the therapists who I thought wanted to see me suffer. However, there was a remarkable twist in all this—the fact that I thought the therapists were out to get me and trying to make me quit actually helped me. I assumed that the better I did, the more likely "those people" would get bored with me and let me leave this terrible place.

My misunderstanding did me a world of good by facilitating more effort from me. In case the therapists or anyone thought I was doing extra work just to come back to who I was before the accident, sorry to disappoint, but my efforts were not put forth to regain what I lost—

they were to get away from "those people."

Now that I fully understand what exactly was going on, I really respect and value the work, effort, and flat-out tenacity the medical staff at UTMC put in on my behalf. I may not have liked it at the time, but I appreciate it immensely now.

6TH INNING

Top of the 6th

Three Strikes: Confusion, Anger, and Pain

March - April 2007

I had not spoken since the accident, nor made any effort to speak. The speech therapists had me try writing. I do not recall even a scrap of anything about my first attempts at writing, but have been told about them, and have read about being in speech therapy and printing my name. Before the accident, my penmanship was poor. After the accident, it was almost illegible.

I had just spent nearly two months being entirely inactive. My dominant right hand was out of practice with just about everything but especially fine motor skills—including penmanship. Having been violently thrown around inside of and then flung out of a bus as it went flying off an overpass, then lying mostly dormant for quite a long time as I healed, my whole body was exceptionally weak and sluggish. In addition to the massive head injuries, systems throughout my whole body had slowed down.

Even a part of my body I would consider too small and insignificant was impacted.

In a properly functioning human body, an epiglottis is a piece of tissue in the throat sealing off the path to anyone's lungs during the process of swallowing. If food or liquid goes into the lungs instead of the stomach, there is a good chance of contracting pneumonia. This simple process was not functioning correctly, which was demonstrated in a swallow test.

Once I became aware we were doing a swallow test, also called a "swallow study," I was not worried. Since my left hand was unusable, I thought the object of the test was to take a drink and not spill anything. The only way I could use my left hand effectively was with help from my right hand. When they gave me the tiny cup of water, I kept this thought in mind and took it with both hands. As cautiously as I could, I took a drink of water. When I did not spill anything, I thought, *Great! Now I can drink water, and I passed the test!*

I found out later this was not true at all. They had me attached to a monitor and after drinking a small amount of water, it was observed that all the water went straight into my lungs. The worst part was that I did not cough or react. Had I been allowed to drink water; the water would have gone straight into my lungs without any cough reflex. Still not completely understanding things at this point, I learned I had failed the thin liquid portion of the test.

This was not the first, second, or maybe even third time I had not succeeded in taking a simple drink of "normal" liquids. I would have to remain on thickener. Feeling miserable and like a total failure, I apologized to Mom. She understood how badly I felt and, through tearful eyes, said, "It's not your fault. There was nothing you could have done to change it."

I told her I wanted to be given another chance to take the test. At the same time, I was thinking, *I can't even swallow water. If I can't even do that, what hope is there for me to be able to do anything else?*

Among probably many other factors, my bland diet may have contributed to the beginning of my weight loss. The fact that I was steadily losing weight concerned my family. I had no idea I was on a special diet, so it wasn't like I was excited to eat anyway. The only reason I ate at all was due to the tremendous appetite I would work up while doing different exercises or being annoyed and confused. However, I also had not been getting enough food since I had been in inpatient therapy.

Finally, my father, Rob, had enough and told the therapists one morning, "We need his weight taken before he does any rehab exercises today."

They weighed me. It was discovered I was losing weight at an alarming rate. On March 1st, at about six feet 2 inches tall, I had boarded the bus weighing a solid and muscular 180 pounds. I weighed in on this day in late April at 125 pounds. At this point, my father informed my head rehabilitation and physical medicine doctor, Doctor Rock. The doctor was very concerned, and food quantities immediately increased, as did my weight, fortunately.

———

An early physical rehabilitation exercise that did the trick in terms of working up an appetite involved me being put in a harness. The harness held me by the waist and shoulders while I was strapped to the treadmill.

I called the harness the "Frankenstein thing." It was designed to support and keep me from falling off the treadmill. A physical therapist on each side of me had to pick up my legs and make them do a walking motion as the machine ran at a snail's pace. Despite what it may have looked like to the unqualified eye, I was not paralyzed—my brain was having a great deal of difficulty communicating with my body.

Consequently, these sessions were more grueling than any workout I had ever experienced as a healthy athlete. Even though the treadmill was at the lowest possible speed, it felt like training for the Olympics.

On one occasion, Dad saw me struggling on the treadmill, even with the physical therapists' help. He told me later, after observing this, he did not have a whole lot of hope that I would walk again on my own. It was a challenging moment for all of us.

Much to my displeasure, the helmet I would wear while exercising made sweat run down my face and into my eyes. There were very few times I could wipe it away. I needed my right hand to grasp the sides of the treadmill.

My left arm and hand were both useless, perpetually locked at an upward diagonal angle against my chest. My left leg had developed foot drop. It was locked, pointing downward, making it impossible to walk without a brace. My left leg, arm, and fingers had all developed spasticity and tone. They were cemented in their respective positions. My left fingers were perpetually clinched in a fist. If I attempted to push my left foot down or pull my left arm away it felt like ripping my muscles. It was agonizing to try to force my left limbs out of their locked positions or unclench my fist.

Once I began to move around regularly, the therapists started to put braces on my left foot and arm to get rid of, or at least minimize, the spasticity and tone. The doctors and staff in Atlanta had attempted to avoid these conditions by telling Karen and Rob to move and exercise my limbs in many ways and from many different angles while I was in a coma. They could move my right-side limbs and had done so faithfully.

They had not been able to, however, move my arm or hand on my left side because of all the broken bones. A physical

86

therapist in Atlanta had also put a boot on my left foot to avoid possible foot drop. I would use my right foot to kick it off because I'm assuming it was uncomfortable. I did this even while in a coma.

Not only did the UTMC staff put braces on my left arm and leg during exercise, but they also put them on in the evening. At least, they "attempted" to. The purpose of putting the braces on at this time of day was so I could have them on all night, and that way the brace would theoretically be working on straightening my limbs while I was supposedly sleeping. You really do not get much sleep in a hospital, but that's beside the point. Befitting an angry and confused former college athlete, usually I struggled and resisted, and every evening became a fight to put these on.

I was wrestling one night with my dad as he was struggling to put on the left arm brace. A nurse saw our battle and said to my dad, "He shouldn't be angry with you—he can be angry with me."

Once the nurse began to grapple with me and the brace, I took a swing at her. I used my good right arm. It is not like me to be violent toward people unless it is in the context of fair play in a sport, but I was in pain, confused, and angry.

I did not land the punch, thank the Lord, but mission accomplished on my end because the nurse said, "Okay, we can leave it off for tonight."

After that incident, medical staff decided to put on casts. Then there would be no fight or struggle to put on braces every night.

I did not understand any of this and why these awful things were happening even though I was being reminded by my parents every night. They would continually remind me night after night, "The Bluffton baseball team got in an accident on the way to Florida. You're in rehabilitation after you were flown up here to The University of Toledo Medical Center. The therapists and medical staff here are trying to help you regain as much as possible of what you lost."

Those descriptions did not stick, so I'd only settle down and understand what was going on and why I was there for maybe a minute or two. After the explanation left my brain, I'd be right back to just as confused as earlier. In those moments, I felt worthless and good for nothing. This was another low point in a long line during my recovery that left me feeling defeated. Still, a different issue had kept me silent.

———

It's not that I had tried to speak and couldn't—it was the thought of speaking did not even occur to me. Most people don't even have to consider they *can* speak, they just do. I did not remember or realize I had a voice and could use it.

I understood instructions, so it was clear the cognition was there, but I just wasn't talking. The hospital had run tests and investigated the reasons behind why. They certainly investigated the health of my vocal cords when they knew breathing tubes had been shoved down my throat amid the emergency. I would imagine they must have also examined any brain damage by looking at scans.

In any case, whatever testing was performed, the hospital had come up with no results. Medical staff had assured my parents, comforting them with statements like, "He'll talk. One day he'll just start talking. We've seen this type of thing before. You'll see, he'll talk."

Days turned to weeks and weeks to over a month without me speaking one word. Mom had resigned herself to the fact I was never going to talk again. Even the hospital had begun to investigate a few different devices that would talk for me. Karen had begun to consider what kind of work I could do someday without a voice. She thought, even though I had lived, that I would not tell the tale—and perhaps she would never hear *my* voice again. It was a grim and puzzling time for many.

None of us knew speech therapy and physical therapy were about to mesh in a most unexpected way. The physical therapists began the serial casting. They would pull out my damaged left limbs and cast them. They would do this periodically, each time pulling my left arm or foot out a little bit closer to a healthy position and cast it. That casting would help loosen the tone and spasticity. This was not a task only requiring treatment once or twice, but rather lasted throughout my entire inpatient stay.

Baseball season was in full swing, flowers were open and blossoming, but I was still in the hospital, unaware of anything in the outside world.

On one of those days in UTMC, which for a remarkably good reason we have documented as May 15th, I was lying on a mat while therapists were trying to stretch my left arm to cast it. I didn't even think about having a voice to use and could only think about the pain. I was pounding the mat with my good right fist to let them know it hurt. Imagine the worst pain you've ever felt. Imagine people you don't know being the source of that pain. Imagine having no idea where you are or why "those people" are messing with you. Now imagine not even considering the fact you are able to use your voice. Though one of my parents—or both—was always in the room for any kind of relatively serious procedure, it never crossed my mind as to why they didn't do anything to help. I just saw them letting this happen and didn't even consider the fact that they weren't helping.

This instance was no exception in terms of my rage and silent agony, and Dad was again present in the room. When he saw me pounding away, he said to me, his voice hopeful, "Son, if it hurts, you can say 'ouch.'"

Apparently, I just needed that cue, because, to the shock of all present, I belted out my first word since the accident: "Ouch!" Appropriate, wouldn't you say?

After my first word on the mat in the middle of May, I had not said anything else for about a week. The entire UTMC staff, motivated by this isolated incident, had been trying anything and everything to get me to speak again. One speech pathologist even told me I could cuss her out for all she cared, just please say something. I wasn't refusing to talk—I just didn't.

Once again, I forgot I had a voice to use. When I had spoken "ouch" on the mat, the cue came from my dad and was combined with incentive from the pain. Without a prompt or intense motivation like unbearable pain, it didn't occur to me to use my voice again.

One day, after Mom dropped me off at the speech room, she was looking forward to getting a bit of a rest in my empty room. Not too long after she arrived, she was summoned back by the speech pathologist, though no explanation was given as to why. While walking down the hall, she remembers wondering why on earth they would call her back when she had just left me there. Was something wrong? Her mind was filled with concern, and she became more and more worried with every step she took.

Shortly after she walked into the speech room, I laboriously pronounced one word to her, "Mom."

In that moment, the tears burst out like a fountain. Though it was my starting-out voice, it was music to her ears. Many of the previous worries about my future dissolved. A whole new door of possible outcomes and options for my future had just been cracked open. Though that door was only just slightly ajar, a part of her concern for my future melted. She knew it was possible for me to improve and advance, and the joy of a mother for her child filled her. I could speak!

This was certainly a major milestone in Karen's mind, but it was unclear if I would remain monosyllabic or be able to speak in conversations again. It was a process and took lots of practice, but slowly I began to do just that. However, it often took some enticing. Since I was not speaking all that much, Dr. Rock came up with a plan. He walked up to my wheelchair in the hallway one day and said to me, "Tim, if you say 'pizza,' I'll buy you a pizza."

Dad was present then, and upon hearing this, knelt behind my wheelchair and whispered, "Say Red Lobster."

In one of if not the first time since the accident, I laughed out loud. Red Lobster is one of my favorite restaurants. In my broken, starting-out voice, I said, "Wed Wobster."

Doctor Rock threw his head back and laughed. True to his word, Doctor Rock gave his resident some money and sent her to buy Red Lobster take out. When I saw them coming with a plastic container that I knew was from Red Lobster, I thought, *Yes! Finally, some real food*!

When I opened the plastic container, much to my dismay, it was pureed pasta shrimp and crab alfredo. I still did not understand why all my food had to be pureed. I thought it was a cruel joke and that, once again, "those people" were having a laugh at my expense and trying to get me to give up. One thing I did learn that day was that, even liquified, Red Lobster food is better than hospital food.

To get me to talk, Doctor Rock had used one of the big motivators for young men my age, food. Doctor Rock believed in me from the first time he looked into my eyes. I would have an appointment with him every three months. At different times, he would inject Botox into my left arm or leg to help loosen the spasticity.

The first time I received a Botox injection I was in my wheelchair with Dr. Rock kneeling in front of me to inject my left foot. He paused and said to his resident, "Maybe you ought to do this, he might kick me." To everyone's shock, I proceeded to fake kick and in happy surprise, Doctor Rock threw his head back laughing again as he handed the needle to his resident.

Doctor Rock believed in me, even if I didn't always see or understand what was going on or what needed to be done at the time to assist in my recovery—which initially was almost everything. Yes, as a medical staff member, he was one of "those people," but I did not deal with him every day, nor was he the person doing the real action of putting me through torture or forcing me out of bed. Every time he spoke or dealt with me, he was assured in his words and invited confidence. I viewed him as on my side because he believed in me, encouraged me, and helped me.

The therapists helped me too, but they were the actual people physically forcing me to complete those tasks or doing what I viewed as torture. Yes, Doctor Rock would order and prescribe those exercises, but I did not see that. So, in this stage of my limited understanding, he was on my side and rooting for me. Before I could even walk or was out of inpatient rehab, he was telling me I would one day drive.

Doctor Rock even offered me a spot in the "Man's Club." I was becoming more familiar with the fact I wasn't good for much and I had notions, as a result, of being an undesirable person. Nobody would want me or need me for anything. I couldn't even stand, couldn't use my left arm, couldn't walk, could barely talk, needed help wiping my own rear-end and was at times drooling. My self-esteem was at an all-time low and being a member of the "Man's Club" made me feel wanted and accepted when I required it most. Doctor Rock would even ask my thoughts over who we should let into the "Man's Club." Yes, it was made up, but it didn't matter. At that time, it was a hundred percent real to me because I needed it to be. Being a member of a club not everyone could be in and having "decision-making authority" gave me somewhere exclusive to belong, just like being a member of a college football or baseball team. In a time of feeling worthless, hopeless, and help-less, being a member of this club felt like acceptance.

Doctor Rock took time to show me great improvements in my progress and made it a point to bring me into the "Man's Club," which helped tremendously in encouraging me. The fact that somebody cared enough about my opinion, even when I was not always cooperative or making sense, felt like accep-tance. Whenever I was speaking with Dr. Rock, it was as if the rest of the hospital did not matter. He listened to me like I was the one in charge and my words carried extreme weight. Sitting directly in front of me, silent, still, all while looking me straight in the eyes. I felt an earthquake could not have shaken his focus on what I was saying. I would often be stumbling through my questions, but he simply waited until I was done and answered. That type of validation—that I mattered—was *critical* to my progress.

———

Physical rehab was hard enough with the treadmill, peg board, doing simple math problems, trying to eat, and anger, but there were other things that confounded and bewildered me. I still had no idea where I was or what was wrong with me. I thought this was all twisted "fun" for these strange people I didn't know—that this was somebody's idea of a sick joke. I knew I used to be able to walk and now for some reason I couldn't. I was sure this whole thing was "those people's" idea of a good time.

I would envision "those people" gathering in the little rooms off the hallway and getting a laugh at how much agony they were putting me through. A laugh at how much I would struggle to do things with my left hand or walk or even stand. I would envision them saying to each other, "Hey, let's strap this loser on the treadmill since he can't walk anymore. Better yet, let's slap a helmet on him so we can watch the sweat roll down into his eyes. It'll be fun to watch him try to wipe his eyes with one hand on the treadmill and the other in a cast. Oh, and just for giggles, let's not tell him what's going on. Won't that be fun!" After they were finished saying those things, I imagined them diabolically laughing.

Time after time, Mom and Dad would explain what was going on. They would constantly be informing me about the bus accident and my injuries. "You have a severe brain injury from the bus accident you were in while you were on your way to Florida with the Bluffton baseball team. You need to relearn basic things to live." They would provide me with descriptions of those things, and other explanations of what I needed to do to recover. Those statements would not stick in my brain for any amount of time.

Back then, the most thinking I could do was limited to what was happening in the present moment.

My thoughts would usually follow a pattern: Get angry at things I did not understand. Forget and move on. Get angry at people who I did not know. Forget and move on. Wonder why I was doing what I was doing. Forget and get hungry. Get mad I couldn't eat right. Wonder why the food was so terrible. Forget and go back to my room. At bedtime, everything would be explained by Mom or Dad yet again.

Then I would attempt to get some sleep, being physically and mentally depleted and hopeless. In the morning, I would wake up having forgotten everything and get enraged and confused all over again.

In the hospital there was no real restful, rejuvenating sleep either, with a nurse coming to check my vitals on the hour. So, sleeping through the night was impossible. Much to my displeasure, it usually wasn't the one I had my "crush" on either that would come check on me. On rare occasions it was her, that made it more tolerable.

I was totally drained. It seemed like I was perpetually attempting to do simple things with great difficulty—these were all easy tasks I used to take for granted. It was continuously degrading to need someone to wipe your rear end when all you knew before was you were a college athlete. It was also exhausting being constantly angry.

One of my biggest internal challenges was losing all control. I had to be helped in showering, eating, wiping my own rear-end, going anywhere, getting dressed—everything I was used to doing on my own. I unknowingly made another helpful choice as inpatient rehabilitation continued. The competitive side of me showed up. I made up my mind to *win* each time I went to exercise. *I'll show them. If I make it look easy, they won't be able to laugh or have such a good time. Maybe they'll get bored and let me get out of this place.*

When the therapists, or "those people," put me on an exercise or weight machine, and told me to do five reps, I'd do eight. If they told me to do eight reps, I'd do ten. I did this not because I somehow knew it would help my recovery, I did this so that I could achieve some sort of control in that moment. If I did less than they said, they would win—if I did more, I would win. All I knew was I didn't like this place. I didn't want to be there, and "those people" were mean to me. I figured the best strategy to leave this place would be to win everything.

Contrary to my thinking, the therapists really were trying to help and had, unbeknownst to me, gotten to know me through Karen and Rob. They learned early on that I was a sports guy and would tailor the rehabilitation exercises around sports. One day, they were working on getting me to stand for long periods of time. They put a *Sports Illustrated* magazine on a small table which could be raised up to standing height. Beyond getting me curious or interested enough to stay standing, this gesture affected my motivation on a deeper level. Reading that magazine and seeing the colorful action shots gave me flashes of who I once had been.

Standing there and looking at the *Sports Illustrated* article about March Madness made me forget where I was. I stood at the table for a long time reading and looking at this magazine, not thinking about anything else. Any thoughts of anger or confusion left me while I was standing at that raised table. I thought of only the article, and it was comforting in the moment. I suppose it would have had the same result, but something tells me the "Swimsuit Edition" was not an option.

Another time, a therapist had a "baseball game" in the hospital lobby. They had a tee set up and rolled my wheelchair to the "batter's box." I took a swing at the ball. Though I could not use my left arm, I used my right arm. I may have taken out some anger on that ball too because I remember smashing it as hard as I could.

One moment I was thinking, *I am so above this. Hitting a stupid ball with a stupid plastic bat, off a stupid tee in the middle of a stupid hospital, from a stupid wheelchair, wearing a stupid helmet. All this garbage is not even close to real baseball. Don't these people know I played college baseball? Don't these people know I played college football?* That aspect, and my overall sense of powerlessness, brought on feelings of hopelessness and desperation beyond anything experienced throughout my entire life.

This circumstance, like many others, was a paradox for me. Immediately after those initial gloomy thoughts, I would enter my competitive sporting mode. With the baseball scenario, for instance, I told myself I was going to do everything in my power to hit the ball as hard and far as I can. Though it wasn't a real ball, and I wasn't standing up, I was back to being my old self for a moment in time, swinging as hard as I could to send that ball as far as possible, to make it difficult to throw me out.

Was I running or going to run? No, but… in those seconds of keeping my eye on the ball, I was who I used to be.

Of course, as soon as the ball flew, I got mad because I couldn't run. Fake baseball, fake bat, fake field. This moment brought victory and defeat, all within a matter of seconds.

In another instance of tailoring my rehabilitation exercises to sports while I was confined to a wheelchair, it was decided I would play "tennis" with an elderly man also in a wheelchair. Each of us had a racket (about the size of a racquetball racket), and the "ball" was a small red balloon.

As we hit the balloon back and forth, it was a paradox of thoughts again. On the one hand, I was playing a sport and thinking, *I'll try to win.* On the other hand, I was in a wheelchair, and good for nothing. Still, this wasn't real equipment. I did not feel like I was really playing a sport, except for one moment when I again had a flashback to who I once was. As we were volleying back and forth, the elderly gentleman hit the balloon back to me lightly and lofted up.

It resembled being set for a spike in volleyball. Being an athlete and competitor, I seized the opportunity and slammed the balloon back since it would mean scoring a "point." When I smashed the soft balloon back, it hit him square in the face. His whole head flew backward, and a clump of his hair lifted off his head and came back down, like a trap door that opens and closes on a hinge. I kind of laughed, although it was more of a chuckle with a grunt. Hey, I scored the point and had victory.

———

The beautiful June weather continued but being in the hospital gave me no sense of the weather or any opportunity to enjoy it. Inpatient rehab dragged on, much to my displeasure.

I do not recall when exactly the following occurrence

happened but do recall the events. On one occasion, my sister, Trisha, was participating in one of my therapy sessions.

An occupational therapist had placed my left arm on a small board with wheels. The object was to swing my left arm across the table to a cone on my right. This may not sound like a terribly difficult task for the average person to accomplish, but my left arm simply would not move. The connections in my brain that talked to my left arm were no longer functioning, at least on that day. In addition, there was still an enormous amount of tone and spasticity inside my left arm, which severely restricted movement.

I was really having a rough time, and Trisha knew it. What she did next was exactly what needed to be done. She went to the front of the table and stooped down. She looked me in the eye and said, "I'm going to beat you, Tim."

She edged her cone across the table with her arm. I looked at my arm holding my cone. It would not move. I willed it to move. It did not move.

Trisha inched her cone closer and closer, all while looking right at me. Challenging me. Inside, I was in a frenzy. I began to sweat. My arm shook from my effort but would not move my cone. My mind screamed, *She's gonna win!* It was almost as if I was caught in a run down or pickle between bases.

In desperation, I reached across and yanked my left arm with my right and finished a second before Trisha. I had beaten her. Trisha smiled at me. She, as well as the therapists and my mom and dad, knew the bigger win. They had witnessed something—my damaged brain could still problem solve.

Inpatient marched on.

———

If Atlanta surgeons had not removed my skull piece, the continued swelling of my brain would have killed me. They froze the removed skull section so that, when the swelling decreased, it could be re-attached. They had scheduled the surgery at UTMC to take place on the three-month anniversary of the crash, and it occurred right on schedule. After the surgery was complete, the surgeon came rushing out of the operating room toward my father. He was, as Dad described him, "as excited as a little kid in a candy shop." He said to Dad, "You must see this!"

The doctor took my dad to a monitor and showed him why he was so excited.

He explained that my brain had stopped swelling. Since the swelling stopped, my brain had also scootched itself away from the hole in the skull because it knew with the hole it was unprotected. My brain had scrunched or shied away from the "danger zone." That an organ in the body can move itself is astounding.

Even more incredible was what happened after the skull piece was replaced. On the surgery recording Rob watched my brain immediately fill back into its old spot. Now that the hole in the skull was covered, it knew it was safe. It's like the brain said, "Okay, my protection is back now—it's safe to return to my usual spot."

When Dad and I talked later, he said the surgeon had told him that, in similar surgeries, sometimes the brain moves quickly, as mine did. Sometimes the brain moves very slowly back, taking whole days or weeks, and sometimes, it doesn't move back at all. After Dad informed me what had happened, I said, "Wow, Dad, so there was nothing that I was injected with or nothing any medical team did in Toledo or Atlanta to cause that?"

"No, nothing anybody did or special medicine they gave you—your brain just moved."

I said, "I'm surprised the surgeon was that excited. He's seen that before."

Dad replied, "Yes, but it was absolutely amazing and miraculous to see it move on the surgery video."

I will never forget how my father described this moment, calling it "the miracle of life."

———

The spring continued to get warmer, and the month summer began that year will always be somewhat of a blur to me. I have no recollection of thoughts about inpatient rehab after my skull piece was replaced. I no longer had to wear the helmet, so I must have been relatively happy, at least about that aspect, but there is not even a scrap of memory regarding any thoughts. I probably just got roused out of bed and was miserable as I was being put through my grueling rehab exercises. I probably quickly forgot that I even had to wear a helmet. That's just a guess.

Mom and Dad had wanted to wait until I was able to understand my circumstances and completely express myself before they explained the full details of the bus accident. If they waited until I was at least consistently and fully talking, they would know more accurately how I took it and that I would be able to retain what was being said. Yes, I was saying words here and there but was a long way from having entire conversations or always being understandable.

On one day in early summer, Mom was sitting beside me on my bed. I shakily stood up and gestured down my body with my good hand. My face implored, *Why am I here?*

Mom knew it was time to tell me the whole story. She went to get Dad, who was out in the hallway. They returned together. I knew something incredibly significant was about to be said as they sat down close to one another looking me in the eye. Both Rob and Karen frowned, and tears formed in their eyes.

Mom asked, "Could I take your hand Tim?"

I slowly put my hand in her hand.

It was as if I had never heard the story before.

Mom began to describe once more everything. "The Bluffton bus got in an accident on the way to Florida. Your bus went flying off an overpass of I-75."

After my initial shock wore off, I wrote on the portable dry erase board, "Was I the worst injured?"

Together they told me, "No. People died, Tim. The bus driver, his wife, and five of your teammates were killed."

They knew I would want to know which teammates. My friend's fiancé had made a scrapbook for me. Mom and Dad showed me the scrapbook, explained everything that had happened, and showed me pictures of the seven people killed.

After hearing the details of the bus crash and the deaths of five of my teammates, I became depressed and felt defeated. Nothing mattered anymore. My regular angry, or insulted, or annoyed thoughts were somewhat insignificant in the grander scheme of these events.

I was in a stupor in the days after being told the terrible details about the accident. I soon began telling myself, *Okay, the next time I go to bed, when I wake up the next day, this will all be just a bad dream. This is the most realistic and longest dream I've ever had but, next time I wake up, it'll all go away.*

As night after night passed and I still woke up in the same situation, I became more and more depressed and downtrodden. I had no desire, no drive, no energy, nothing. Everyone did their best to help me. My sister, Trisha, tried to challenge me to race cones again, but I simply did not care. My brain was severely injured and now my heart was broken.

I had known those guys. I had seen them run, seen them throw, heard them speak. Then the questions began. *Why had I lived, and not them? How can somebody get thrown out of a bus flying off an overpass of I-75 at highway speed, land on the pavement and still be alive? Why had I not been paralyzed?*

What had I done to deserve these life-altering injuries? What had I done to deserve to live? All those young men had just as much right to survive as I did.

Of course, none of these questions had answers, or were necessary, but that was my state of mind.

The hospital staff on the floor all noticed that I was extremely down, much more so than usual. Two nurses decided to try to help. Before even entering my room, they laid out on a wheeled gurney and sailed by the doorframe. Next, they surfed into my room on that gurney and began to lip sync and dance to a song. It was incredibly goofy with some awkward dancing, but they accomplished their mission. I started to chuckle and cheer up a tad. That's what nurses are supposed to do—help the patient. They decided to help me as their patient in a way perfect for the moment.

Just like James in Atlanta, these two nurses went out of their way without any extra compensation to give me the best chance to recover. I needed energy for rehabilitation exercises, and the feelings of depression were draining all my drive and spirit—which was already largely diminished in numerous other ways. My fuel tank was getting very close to empty. Those nurses noticed and did what they could to help. As members of my team, they were giving their all for my recovery.

———

Dad may not recall all the exact details of the following anecdote, but he does recall what his reinvigorating moment was.

Inpatient rehab at UTMC is about a forty-minute drive from my parents' house in Ida, Michigan. While I was at UTMC inpatient, my parents, at separate times, were able to go home and rest, shower, and recharge. The "reinvigorating or reviving moment" for Rob happened to take place on a day he was home, enjoying one such rest-and-recharge occasion as much as he could considering the circumstances. Right at a period when dad's energy was severely dwindling, he experienced something unexpected.

Dad is very big into gardening and has what is often referred to as a "green thumb." Our yard is filled with many kinds of plants and flowers, and he enjoys tending to them.

On this unique day, he stood at our kitchen window looking into our backyard. He noticed the Rose of Sharon bush he had planted years before, since it was straight out from the window. As he observed, he realized half the bushes branches were dead, but the other side was in full bloom. Rob thought, *I didn't think that was two plants—I could have sworn that was a single bush.*

Dad went out for a closer look. He dug down around the trunk, expecting to see two separate trunks. He kept digging until it became obvious there was a single trunk. He figured if one side is dead, the whole plant must be dead, and the other side would soon follow. He made a mental note to dig it up when he had more time.

Standing back and looking at it, he thought, *That plant is kind of like Tim. One side is good, and the other side is dead. That's sad, because it was a beautiful plant while it was fully alive, just like Tim had a lot going for him when he was fully healthy.*

About a week later, Rob had still not gotten around to digging up the plant. In the meantime, there was some major gain in my rehab. My guess is it had to do with my speech, because I did not have any noticeable major gains while in inpatient other than improvement with talking.

When he got home that day, Dad noticed the same plant but this time it stood out in another distinct way. The "dead" side of the plant was filled in and was almost as if it had been growing at the same rate as the other side all along. After observing this and remembering the comparison to me with one side of the plant being dead since half of me was basically unusable, Dad immediately looked to the sky and said, "Thank you, God. Tim's going to be okay."

He did not know to what extent I would recover, the timeline, or anything else specific about my recovery, but that occurrence told him I was going to be okay.

When it became imminent that I was soon going to be leaving inpatient, my mother was on a computer in the lobby of the hospital rehab floor at UTMC. She was researching different group homes where I could live after being released from inpatient, because the prognosis was not good in terms of my mobility and overall independence. A caring staff member soon came up to her, inquiring about what she was checking.

Within a day the staff approached her about the possibility of my coming home instead—they strongly felt I would blossom in my home environment and receive better care there. Emotionally, there is nothing like recovering in your home and sleeping in your own bed.

The staff understood this was not an easy solution for the Berta family. My parents would have to be educated for my care and our home inspected. I would need to come to outpatient rehab at least three days a week. My food would still need to be pureed and my drinks thickened. They would also have to make physical accommodations to our home, altering some things to suit my needs. A raised toilet seat and shower bench would need to be installed along with a ramp for entering and exiting our front door with the wheelchair.

Mom listened carefully and understood the immense burden it would be for my entire family. Knowing this, she still accepted the challenge for my benefit. She hadn't considered the option of my coming home because it had simply seemed daunting and even impossible, but now there was a way.

It may very well be that I get my unwillingness to resign in the face of difficulty or failure from Mom and Dad—neither of my parents will back down from a challenge, especially when it comes to their children. That is real love, and I do not have the proper vocabulary to describe what that kind of support means to me. This incredible support continued to push me toward a victory.

Bottom of the 6th
Personal Reflections

Some of the stories from inpatient rehabilitation make me sick to my stomach to hear. I don't know how I or my family got through the many scares and challenges. The thought of that is nauseating. The following story serves as an example of how easily everything could have gone badly for me.

I had needed a machine to breathe for me in Atlanta, and Rob and Karen thought the plan was not to send me on the flight to Toledo until I could breathe on my own. For some reason, this strategy was not followed. I was flown up to UTMC still needing breathing assistance. UTMC then formulated their own initial design of reteaching me how to breathe on my own. Their original plan was to narrow down the size of the breathing tube hole in my neck through gradual healing of the skin. They would use smaller and smaller breathing tubes until tubing was no longer necessary.

In any case, years after I had been discharged from inpatient, I learned I had knocked out my breathing tube early on during that inpatient stay. I'm not clear on when exactly this happened, but thankfully, after it was knocked out, it did not need to be reinserted.

Stories like those make me realize how blessed I was to

have this whole situation go as it did. At any given time when the breathing machine was operating and very much needed, it could have been accidentally knocked out, by me or anybody else. At any time when my vitals were off, a mistake could have been made. And during that time when I was rapidly losing weight, my dad may not have fought so hard for me. All types of things could've easily gone wrong, and the result would have been that I would not be here, or where I am today. That's incredibly humbling. I know God was on my team.

Our bodies were designed to function in perfect timing and harmony. When one system in the body is off, it may cause a lot of issues. The epiglottis being impacted is something I never even considered as a possible injury. I did not know how important it is to have a functioning epiglottis until mine was compromised. I absolutely detested having to eat pureed food and drink thickened liquids.

Now, even fully understanding why the food had to be pureed and why my drinks had to be thickened, it's still not a good memory. I mean, yes, thank you to the hospital for not killing me, but that realization still brings no solace when I reflect on the misery that mealtime was to me then. Mealtime has been one of my favorite times of day my entire life, so after I had this realization, it was like another major joy of my life had been stolen.

Another painful and confusing situation pertaining to my recovery was the condition of my entire left side. I did not understand why my left leg and arm were tight, or why my hand was clinched, or what had to be done to at least improve those conditions as much as possible. It is baffling those conditions came but is equally unbelievable that even while in a coma when I had been in Atlanta, I kicked the boot off. I also can't believe I "forgot" for a while that I had a voice to use.

Since I was not talking a whole lot, I was frequently alone

in thought and would be stewing and contemplating various ideas and feelings.

By the evening, I would always completely forget all "those people" trying to have fun at my expense throughout the course of the day. These evening thoughts seemed more focused and detailed because I was not constantly distracted by being told to perform tasks or being given something I was supposed to eat. Maddeningly there appeared to be no end goal or finish line, which was truly a hopeless feeling. The thoughts I experienced would have my wheels rotating endlessly.

Why did this happen to me? Why was I the worst one injured? How could this happen to me? What have I done to deserve this? Did I not work hard at anything I did? What good is all this exercising stuff doing? People keep saying they're praying for me, but I just don't feel it. I can't walk or move my left arm anymore and never will be able to—that's just the reality of it. Might as well get used to it. I know what it is—why I am like this now—I just did not work hard enough, and God is mad at me.

God you could fix all of this immediately if you wanted to and you don't so I must have done something to deserve this. I know I don't always behave myself or do what I'm supposed to do. Wait a minute, what about murderers who get away with what they've done, never to face consequences? Or what about the night I saw a group of guys getting wasted and bringing girls back to their rooms then bragging about it? I never did anything like that. And when I did naughty things, they positively weren't any worse than anyone else did and I certainly didn't brag about them.

Well, if you're mad at me, God, then I'm mad at you. So there. This doesn't happen to everyone, and this is NOT fair. I worked just as hard as anyone else. What kind of a God who is supposed to love me or act in my best interest would let this happen? It sure doesn't seem like you have a good plan for me after all. God, if you hold everything in your hands, then where were you when my world completely fell apart?

Often it felt like God had abandoned me. But now that I see how everything was working together, I know that God was right there.

Also, like most everyone else, I do not remember anything about my first word as a baby. I'm told it was "dada." I vaguely remember the situation of saying my second first word "ouch" from discussing this instance with my family often, and how I felt. It hurt.

The feelings of pain and being under attack had brought out that word, along with Dad reminding me I could speak. I do not remember speaking to Mom in the speech room or how it must have impacted me. I can only imagine how it impacted Mom to hear her child speak when she was resigned to the fact that she would never hear my voice again. Dad may have had those same concerns. Out of love and maybe desperation, he reminded me I could speak while I was laying on the mat. And I did.

Additional evidence of my brain function included the fake kick. I had heard his words, my brain had processed them and sent the message to my body to tease the doctor with a fake kick, and I could. That moment was dripping with hope, and as Doctor Rock would say later, in that moment among many others, he knew I was in there, trapped inside my injured brain. I remember another time, during one of our therapy appointments, he had me walk down a hallway. Throwing his hands up, he stated, "Tim, I didn't even think you'd make it this far. I have never seen this."

I was sent to UTMC for a reason, and one reason may have been the high-quality staff. Along with Doctor Rock, "those people" were the therapists at UTMC. They took the time to get to know me through talking with my family and looking at my scrapbook. One therapist asked if she could take my scrapbook home overnight. This displays their dedication in learning about me.

The way they tailored my rehab to sports was brilliant. Getting me to play baseball and tennis, and using the *Sports Illustrated* magazine to encourage me to stay vertical for an extended period are wonderful examples of their creativity and investment in my outcome. Looking back, I deeply appreciate what they did and the efforts they went through on my behalf. Even though at the time I hated them because I did not understand.

Nobody knows you better than your family, and my sister was, and still is, no exception. Trisha knew I was a competitive person. She knew how to "speak" to me. Trisha also knew the therapist was trying to get me to move my left arm. She knew I wanted to and was trying my best. She helped me in the best way she knew. Trisha was MVP that day.

God was also "speaking," and, this time, it wasn't from a bush. When I learned about my brain moving and what Dad said about watching it move, I saw God again. My brain moving on its own after the skull piece was replaced is just like Dad said— "the miracle of life."

I had studied biology, physiology, organic chemistry, and other life sciences in advanced high school courses and at the college level, but I had absolutely no idea that type of mysterious power—a human organ shifting away from potential danger of its own volition—could be demonstrated in just such a way. Talk about a wake-up call.

To be perfectly clear, I'm not saying God looked down at that specific moment and caused my brain to move—I'm saying the brain moved on its own because it was designed with that type of power already in it.

Another wake-up call came from learning the full details of the bus accident. The worst thing about being told that story was that there was nothing I could do. It happened and it was done. There was no going back in time, no hitting "Reset" on the game system—this was real life, and I had no other option but to deal with it.

Guilt also came along with the questions. The more I learned about what happened, the guiltier I felt. I was constantly thinking and asking why those young men died while I lived. This question haunts me every single time I am reminded of the accident, which is every day. There are reminders every time I see the trach scar in my neck or the scar on the side of my head. Every time I'm facing a difficult challenge or am completely worn out, I think of my fallen teammates.

This is not to say there were not some personal good moments that came out of this. My friend's fiancé making that scrapbook is one of the kindest things anyone has ever done for me. I have seen and heard about the outpouring of love for me and my family from the community and even from complete strangers. They were all there in big and little ways and even the most heartfelt thank you from me would not even begin to cover the enormousness of their support.

I've often heard the saying "the devil is in the details," but in my recovery, God was in the details. Along with allowing Mom to pick out the correct medical instrument on the plane, God spoke to Dad and Mom in their own unique ways. To this day, Dad refers to that Rose of Sharon plant as his "burning bush." Just as God spoke to Moses through a burning bush, Dad feels God was speaking to him through his Rose of Sharon bush. Interestingly, just like fragile vocal cords easily damaged when shoving breathing tubes down somebody's throat during an emergency, Rose of Sharon petals are incredibly delicate like crepe paper. By the dead side quickly filling in with white blooms, Dad knew I was going to be okay.

When somebody saw my mother researching different homes to send me, staff soon approached her with the idea of me returning home and coming for outpatient rehab. They were one hundred percent correct.

I can see God orchestrating that detail, since looking back on the whole journey I improved immensely once I was out of the hospital environment and in outpatient. Being in my home habitat and sleeping in my own bed did wonders for my mental and physical health.

During that time before I could come home, I cannot imagine what my parents went through daily, knowing their son was in the fight of his life, quite literally fighting *for* his life, yet they could do nothing except support him and pray. But, in the end, it was that support and prayer that saved me.

7TH INNING

Top of the 7th
Return from a Long Road Trip
June - October 2007

I woke on June 21, and soon realized today was the day. I mentally prepared myself to begin a new phase of my life. The day I had been longing for since waking up in Toledo many weeks ago had finally arrived, I was going home and leaving this place of torment.

I already had experienced a brief taste of home a few days beforehand. My parents, a couple hospital staff, and therapists had gone for an inspection to look at what would be needed for me to live at home, and I rode along with them. A hospital van had taken the group. I was loaded and unloaded while remaining in my wheelchair.

As we pulled in the driveway, the familiar earthy smell of the country and sight of Dad's landscape made me forget I was in a hospital van. Once we got inside the house, hospital staff and therapists inspected my home for possible essential accommodations, informing my parents what was going to be necessary. Like a ramp for entry into the front door, a raised toilet seat, a shower bench, clear furniture for the wheelchair, etc. I was just wheeled to my room. The rehab aide unloaded me into my bed, and I fell asleep as he sat at my bedside. I had forgotten how good my bed felt. Much to my displeasure, the time soon came for me to be forced out of my bed and forced to travel back to the hospital. That memory was just that, a memory and brief taste of what was to come. But on this specific day, I knew I was leaving the hospital and would stay home.

I had made it a goal on the day I was leaving the hospital for good to walk to the car. I was very much looking forward to that sort of cathartic moment, but, unfortunately, protocol required that any patient leaving must be rolled out in a wheel-chair. When I learned this, I needed to make a new goal. The revised goal was to walk across the rehab gym to tell "scrubs lady" goodbye. She had been the therapist that worked with me the most.

On the day I was leaving for good, she stood waiting for me at the other end of the small inpatient rehab gym. She did not move closer or make it easier for me to approach her, which made accomplishing this goal all the sweeter. Mom walked beside me, having been trained on how to catch me or get me off the floor in case I fell. It was a very slow process. I didn't fall or require my mom's assistance, much to her joy. I was elated to achieve this milestone. A victory was won.

Dad went out to bring our van to the front entrance. This time, I really knew I'd get to stay home, so as I was wheeled to the car, my heart was as light as air, but soon realized the rest of my body was not light at all.

I struggled and strained to help as I was entering our family van. It was a painful discernment but shortly realized in the "real world" I was cumbersome and clumsy. As a former college athlete, this was a foreign, scary feeling. With this unexpected effort, all the joy and anticipation of getting out of this terrible place left me. I thought, *How am I going to function in the outside world if I can't even get into a van?*

I became completely focused on lifting and moving my legs while trying to keep balance—there was no room in my head for anything else. Physically, it was draining just to lift my legs. It felt as though each had an immeasurable weight still strapped to them.

The "old Tim" would have jumped in the front seat, slammed the door, and buckled the seat belt in one fluid motion. This "new Tim," whom I was still getting to know and trying to understand, had to lean on the side of the front seat and then one at a time lift his legs up high enough to get in. The "real world" quickly had me physically exhausted and mentally drained. And we had not even left the parking lot.

I was given about a week off from rehab to recuperate and transition. This would also help my family get acclimated to what needed to be done to take care of me. A ramp had been constructed to assist me in entering through the front door with my wheelchair. Upon entering, my sisters, Trisha and Tonya had a handmade sign with different colored letters hung up that read, "WELCOME HOME TIM!" That sign was hung for me to see right as I entered the front door. They may not realize it, but I still frequently think back on the feeling of welcome and love from both.

I'm sure feeling welcomed and loved also contributed to the sudden shift in my sleep quality. I have never slept as well as I did on the first night of being home. I remember the first moment when I was lying in my own bed and knew, really *knew*, that I was home for good. I was laying there thinking, *this has got to be a dream.*

On this occasion, it was a good dream and not a nightmare. It was wonderful, comfortable, joyous, and peaceful all wrapped into one. This was a different variety of excitement though because this excitement did not keep me awake—it put me to sleep. I'm guessing I went to bed that night at around 9:30 or 10:00. I slept, and slept, and slept, and when I first even moved the next day, it wasn't until around three or four in the afternoon. Talk about a refreshing night's sleep.

When I didn't even budge for that huge stretch of time, Mom tells me she began to grow concerned. She had just come from a place where she had constant awareness of my body health stats—a place where I was monitored night and day. Now, she had nothing but the sound of my steady breathing as I snoozed away.

She wasn't sure if I was going to wake up.

After I did arise—much to my mother's relief—I was completely famished. With help, I was transferred from my bed into the wheelchair and wheeled out into the kitchen for breakfast.

Well, given the time of day, it was more like an afternoon snack or early dinner. I was overjoyed with the hopes of this food being much better. While in the hospital many reasons probably contributed to the fact that I did not realize my food had to be pureed and liquids thickened. As I watched my mom preparing my meal by dumping it into a blender, I was devastated.

Karen explained why my food needed to be blended and why a thickener packet had to be squeezed into my drink. It felt as though a screaming line-drive had hit me square in the mouth. This was not at all what I had hoped or longed for. I now realized how much more of a fight I had in front of me. Talk about a major letdown. It felt like all the chaos, anger, and confusion from inpatient rehab had followed me home.

I felt defeated again. Despite the love and support of my family, coming home seemed just a little less special once I was confronted with this new reality. It was like part of the hospital

—which I'd hoped to shrug off completely—had followed me home.

I'm guessing my dismay and disappointment was written all over my face, and that my parents could see it. Honesty and being up front was the only way they operated with their children, and knew they needed to act no different here.

Dad must have told me something like this before while in the hospital, but this is the first time these words really stuck in my brain. In a matter of fact loving tone, he said, "As unfair as this is and as terrible a feeling as this must give you, you didn't cause this mess, but you and only you must do the grunt work to get yourself out. You have every right to be angry and bitter, but only you can fix this. Your Mom and I, along with countless others, can drive you places, cheer you on, help you to do certain things, pray for you and give you all the love we know how, but only you can fix this."

This time, his words resonated. He was doing what Mom did years before when I had talked with her about not making the basketball team—giving it to me straight and telling me like it is.

I didn't like not being able to drive, I didn't like not being able to walk, and I didn't like having to drink thickened liquids or eat puréed food. I finally somewhat understood the size of the mountain there was to climb, and I recognized that, if I wanted to climb it, only I could put in the physical work. There was no guarantee any of my efforts would produce any improvement either, regardless of how strenuous or challenging they were. Such is the nature of brain injuries.

I also credit Dad for asking the doctor, at each appointment, what medications I could discontinue—something I didn't even consider. Each appointment would start with Dad asking, "Well, what pill can we lose next?"

Doctor Rock was on board and eliminated medication after medication. From Rob's viewpoint, the fewer drugs I was on the better, and Doctor Rock agreed. Dad was another member of my team fighting to give me the best chance at recovery and victory.

During outpatient, we still went to appointments with Doctor Rock every three months. In our appointments, he often would ask what I had for breakfast. Sometimes I would remember, sometimes I wouldn't, but what I thought was just friendly conversation was him monitoring and checking my recall and brain function.

———

Since I was home to stay now, it was time to begin my outpatient therapy at UTMC. Because of the forty-minute drive from our home in Ida, Michigan, doctors in Atlanta had selected The University of Toledo Medical Center. Initially, my doctors had wanted me to stay in Atlanta and attend The Shepherd Rehab Center, but UTMC was performing a lot of the same rehabilitation techniques Shepherd was doing. In fact, come to find out, on the day of the accident, there had been UTMC therapists at The Shepherd Rehab Center learning some of their practices. Now that we were back home, all we had to do each rehab day was get to UTMC.

Getting to UTMC was not as easy as it sounded. Initially, my appointments had been set for early morning. I don't know if that was a factor in this near disaster, but it was more than likely what is next described. I had just spent about fifteen weeks laying on my back and, as we neared the hospital, I began to feel sick to my stomach. Not from nerves, but from the motion of a moving vehicle and trying to eat at the same time. We had been awake early enough but had not anticipated getting me ready would take such a long time. It was painfully slow to even get the forty-minute trip to the rehabilitation hospital started.

First, we had the challenge of getting me out of bed, using the toilet, brushing my teeth, and dressing me. All of which I needed massive assistance with. Second, it took time loading me, loading the wheelchair, and getting all the assorted braces, getting the thickened juice bottle for when I took a drink (I could not just drink water out of a drinking fountain), and packing other assorted things since we had no idea what to expect.

My mother was driving, I was in the front passenger seat, and my sister, Tonya, was in the back seat trying to spoon feed me breakfast since we ran out of time to eat. Mom had thought it'd be a good idea to have an extra set of rehab clothes along too and had packed some. It's a good thing she did.

When we were within a few minutes of the hospital, I felt sick, and warned, "I'm going to throw up!"

Mom quickly spotted a parking lot and whipped in. As I began to vomit, Tonya, who was seated directly behind me, swiftly grabbed the trash basket from the middle console and wrapping her arms around the front seat, attempted to hold the basket under my mouth.

As most people know, it's hard to aim vomit. Some of it got onto Tonya's arms, and she handled it like a trooper. The good news, too, was that mom had brought along that extra bag of rehab clothes. I was able to be changed in the UT parking lot, since we had another set of hands in the form of Tonya.

We still made it to rehab.

To this day, I am grateful to Tonya for her help. She was on my team, and just like James in Atlanta helping to clean my room and keep my environment as hygienic as possible, or the nurses dancing in Toledo working to cheer me up, Tonya did what she could to give me the best chance at success. Because of her selfless assistance—the fact that she had come along and chose to be present—we did not have to cancel my first day of outpatient rehab.

A staff member in the outpatient rehab reception office had walked into the bathroom while Karen was at the sink cleaning vomit off the clothes I had been changed out of. After that staff member asked what she was doing and mom explained, the staff member smiled, and mom returned a smile, albeit probably a fake one. Not sure if that was a factor in deciding, but after that incident, my outpatient schedule was reworked so that it would take place in the afternoons, three days a week starting at 1 p.m.

My mother would go to her job in the morning and arrive home about noon to drive me to therapy. I realize how taxing this must have been for her, to give up a half day's pay three times a week. That is pure love for your child, and my mom was then, always has, and always will be, on my team.

Each time I went to rehab, I went through a combination of speech therapy, occupational therapy, and physical therapy. In the first year of my outpatient rehab, I had an additional hour of therapy with a social worker for weekly counseling. The counseling helped me deal with the loss and mental trauma my nervous system had been experiencing over the past months.

The counselor helped me look at what I still had rather than what I lost, and we talked about trying to find joy in everyday things. Hearing someone on the outside of my circle talk about that concept was helpful to me. Now that I completely understood everything that was really going on, I had just been stewing over the great life I had lost and the unfairness of it all. Looking at what I still had—or what I had an opportunity to relearn—was a true refreshment.

The more I thought about it and the more I learned about what happened, the more grateful I became. No scientific evidence was present to affirm how I had miraculously survived such an ordeal. My doctors had told me that scientifically I should not even be alive. I tried to be grateful for this as often as possible.

Most of the time, Mom took me to rehab, but sometimes she would need to stay at work and a home care worker would drive. Other times, Uncle Troy and Aunt Kay would take me and, on his days off, Dad would drive there.

On this day, Mom had taken me, and the scenario that would play out would contribute greatly to my sense of gratefulness.

One day, I was in the speech therapy room, which was a small room off the larger main gym. There was a violent bang on the door. The speech therapist got up, cracked open the door, said a few words, and came back. A few minutes later, we finished, and she began to wheel me out to my mother. As we passed through the rehab gym, a man was standing at the entrance to the lobby. Once he saw me, he started pointing and yelled, "Hey, you! What's that thing?"

At first, I was unsure what he meant, and I shrugged. Thinking, *I don't know what you mean, and besides, who the heck are you? Why are you pointing and yelling at me?*

Karen was nearby, hearing all this. She told me later that she had considered intervening but then told herself, *He's going to have this type of thing happen on occasion and needs to learn how to deal with it on his own. If things get bad, I'll step in, but I'll see how he handles it.*

The man continued. "You know!" Shaking his pointing finger at me all the harder, he added, "That hole in your neck!"

At this point, the speech therapist, sounding exasperated, reminded me of the tracheotomy scar in my neck. I hesitantly informed the man, "That scar is from the trach I had to help me breathe immediately following my accident." I smugly thought this would satisfy him.

Instead, he yelled again, "Well, you should cover it up!"

I shook my head, shrugged again, and proudly said, "My trach hole? No way, women think they're sexy." Then I smiled politely and, pointing to him, added, "Maybe you should get one."

Upon hearing this, the man grunted, turned, and stormed off.

I grinned, and Mom was cracking up. She knew I'd be able to handle myself and was thankful.

"Well, you haven't lost your sense of humor," she said.

It's important to understand this patient also had a brain injury. My brain injury was the worst anyone can suffer, so if his wasn't as bad, that simply means it was considered less severe.

At the same time, all brain injuries are different. While I lost the ability to speak for some time, and the motor skills connection, the man who pointed out my trach might have lost his social filter. Doctors in Atlanta had told my parents that, once I came out of this, I might start swearing, carrying on, and not be myself. I very easily could have had that happen and acted in such a way toward anybody, too. The fact I didn't gives me more reason to be grateful, and I had a whole lot of other events to be grateful for as well.

Early during my outpatient therapy years, another dramatic event took place. One that aided healing in a colossal way. There was a local deep tissue therapeutic masseuse who had seen my story on the news and had told herself, "I know I can help that man."

After a few months, she hadn't got around to figuring out how to contact me. Just like others, her life had become busy, and reaching out had slipped her mind. A short time after, my aunt, Lucy, was prescribed deep tissue massage and was referred to her. As they were talking about a variety of general things, their conversation somehow turned to "the guy in that terrible bus accident." Aunt Lucy then told her "that guy" was her nephew. The masseuse then told herself, "If that's not God calling me, I don't know what is."

She contacted me and, for about the span of a year, gave me a one-hour deep tissue massage every week at no charge. It was documented in my medical records that deep tissue massage, paired with my other therapies, brought me further down the recovery road.

About seven months after the accident the swallow test was repeated, following the same procedure as the previous ones I had taken. However, the results of this test were remarkably different.

It was concluded I no longer had to eat pureed food. I loved Red Lobster, and it was the restaurant Doctor Rock had used to reward me for speaking. It only seemed like a good fit to go there and celebrate. Finally, after eating a strict, pureed diet for half a year, that season had ultimately passed.

The Red Lobster food was just as good as I had remembered it being. Every bite was a splash of flavor beyond any meal I had indulged in for quite some time. In fact, it felt as though this food was new and a fresh new experience for my taste buds. I was especially overjoyed to know—and to taste— that this food had not been puréed and shaped to resemble solid food. I was able to eat it as it was meant to be enjoyed. Plus, I was not eating inside of the hospital surrounded by a bunch of people whom I thought were bent on making my life miserable. All this just made the food taste even more incredible.

It was just my immediate family with me that day—Mom, Dad, Trisha, and Tonya—and it was quite a celebratory evening. My amazing gift, beyond a doubt, was being *inside* a Red Lobster restaurant, smelling and tasting pleasant food instead of hospital crud, and munching on my feast. The shrimp were whole, the crab pieces were in lumps the way they should be, and the clams inside the clam chowder were intact.

Following my outpatient occupational therapist's advice, I sat with exceptional posture, chewed the food extra well, and tucked my chin to my chest while swallowing. Using this strategy, I was able to tolerate eating my entire meal, and even added a dessert. This was a moment of pure victory! However, even victory has its casualties, and I still had to bring into the restaurant thickened liquids to drink. I almost always drank thickened Gatorade since water did not taste like water when the thickener packet was added. Still, this was a well-earned victory.

———

Before the accident, Mike Smith, my friend and Bluffton football teammate, had asked me to be one of his groomsmen at his wedding. I was now in a wheelchair, however, and I hoped I would still be participating—not all venues are meant for people in wheelchairs, and I didn't want to be a burden on anyone's big day either.

When I learned I was in fact still going to be a groomsman at the wedding, a plot began to form. During rehearsal, I did not stand out of the wheelchair as the bride, Molly, came down the aisle. I wanted to surprise Mike and Molly for their wedding, which had been scheduled a few weeks after Labor Day, the year of the accident.

At the wedding, as the music for the bride's entrance began, I looked around, making sure everyone in the audience was turned to her. Once certain everyone had their eyes on Molly, I slowly and shakily stood out of the wheelchair. Fellow groomsmen were on either side of me, just in case. I had practiced getting out of the wheelchair and standing in rehab but did not want any attention focused on me: this was their day. I remained standing for her the whole trip down the aisle but was glad to sit down when she got to the altar. My mission was accomplished, and I had my victory. This victory was for Molly and Mike.

Since another football teammate and I were co-best men, we each proposed a toast. For my toast, I read some lyrics from the song "My Wish" by Rascal Flatts. I had practiced beforehand so I could talk as clearly and coherently as possible. When the toast came, I was desperately trying to pronounce each word. My talking was very slow since I had just started using my voice regularly. As far as I could tell, everyone understood what I was saying. Another victory had been won.

At the reception, the thrill of victory quickly turned into what I perceived as defeat. I felt unwanted again, and on the dance floor sidelines. Throughout my entire life, I had loved to dance, and now I was unable to.

As you can imagine, being in a wheelchair does not make dancing the same. At the bride garter toss, I felt worthless, figuring there'd be no hope of catching that thing. I was in a wheelchair with everybody surrounding me. I felt defeated.

Dancing as I did before the accident was out of the question and might always remain that way. I had struggled to stand out of my wheelchair and slow dance with my platonic date. She was a gal I had been friends with at Bluffton. I may have stolen her key card as a prank one night too, but let's not get into that...

Still, I could barely move without losing my balance. The faster variety of dancing was hopeless. But I still wanted to at least pretend to be dancing. Sitting in the wheelchair, I waved and shook my arms. It wasn't the same and taking up a lot of space on the floor felt awkward and burdensome.

Then it began. All the bridesmaids circled around me and started to dance, shaking their hips, jumping, shouting, and taking pictures of each other and with me. I felt accepted and wanted with these numerous college-aged females dancing in a circle around me while in my wheelchair.

In this moment, I was no longer a severely disabled undesirable loser. I was a highly desired college athlete who had just experienced yet another victory. The big success was in reclaiming yet another part of myself (even if only for a moment) that I thought had been lost.

———

After the weekend wedding, it was back to rehab three days a week. At this point it had been about eight months since the accident, and my team's plan was to bring my functionality as close to what it was before the accident, which meant we needed to retest my cognition.

Nobody knew to what extent my healing brain would allow me to recover or where the ending point would be. I was not even sure if I'd be able to function day to day on my own, but I didn't think much about that until the neuropsychological evaluation scheduled for late October that year. I was given what was at the time the standard neuropsychological tests given to all patients with brain injuries.

A friendly doctor giving this psychological exam asked me numerous questions, told a story I would attempt to repeat back to her later, gave me different mental logic puzzles to solve, and had presented me with a host of other assorted general material tests—tests a twenty-two-year-old with eight weeks remaining before graduating with a Bachelor of Arts in Biology degree should certainly have been able to breeze through.

During the test and unbeknownst to me at that time, she had carefully observed and recorded my reflexes, eye movements, and reaction times. The testing had taken the better part of a day and had left me entirely drained.

I had felt a bit disappointed—I was certain I had not done as well as I thought I could have or should have on a few memory tests but wasn't too worried. After all, I had bigger things to worry about regarding the physical aspects of my recovery. Having a limited understanding of what I had been through, I certainly thought I was above these tests.

About a week later, outpatient rehab continued, and I got scheduled to review the results of these tests. Tests that my mom and I thought would modify or even enhance the blueprint for my recovery.

The day of the results assessment, Mom glides my wheelchair on the carpeted floor as we approach the outpatient rehabilitation gym. Her footsteps are steady as she pushes me along. As we wheel into a small separate room just off the large outpatient rehab gym, my mind is racing, as well as my mind can race, that is.

Now, as Mom wheels me into the small room, I notice the friendly doctor who gave me the test sitting against the back wall. Mom places me in front of a desk.

On the other side of the desk is a woman whom I have never seen before. This woman looks at Mom and me with something akin to total apathy. It occurs to me that she hadn't been the one to administer the test, nor had anything to do with any of my earlier rehab treatment. She begins giving us the test results in a voice so void of emotion she could have been a computer. My road to recovery abruptly turns into a dead end.

The test results are dismal.

"These results display a complete lack of brain awareness or plasticity, and so for life you will not be able to learn anything else. You are not going to finish your degree and certainly will never become a nurse, let alone a nurse anesthetist. How does that make you feel?", she asks. Surprising mom and I with a heartless edge to her voice. She moves on with such speed I have no time to respond.

I squirm a bit but keep myself from showing any reaction—my brain needs time to process her words. I am trying to wrap my mind around not being able to finish college or learn anything new.

My present situation is my final state, according to this expert.

Inside, I am reeling from the blow. I think, *Wait, don't you know I was on spring break in my senior year of college? That I was eight weeks away from completing one phase of my career and life goals? Doesn't that mean anything to you?*

My brain, apparently working better than she thinks it is, is translating thoughts into feelings, and I react. Inside, my heart drops to my stomach as I mentally attempt to grasp what she is saying. I have had this crushing feeling before, so I don't visibly react. This is made easier since my brain needs time to absorb and take everything in. It's as if I can feel nearby thunder rumbling inside my chest.

She moves the conversation—so far, a very one-sided discussion with outcomes set in stone—into the reaction-time and eye-movement portion of the test results. Apparently, I scored exceptionally low on those as well because she tells me I will never be able to drive a car.

My shaking voice threatens to give me away, but I ask anyway, "Now, you mean for one or two years, right?"

Her response is a matter of fact, icy-cold word that sends chills down my spine. "Never. How does that make you feel?" she asks again.

With my lips slightly apart, I sit there motionless. Any life in my eyes had just been drained. My mouth and arms do not move but my stomach seems to jump into my throat as I try to absorb this unanticipated punch to the gut.

Her indifferent tone makes me feel like I am being attacked. I can't trust myself to speak again without letting loose a tirade of words I may regret. I bite my tongue. Inside, my mind is speeding from thought to thought as if being flung around by a tornado, but I refuse to give her the satisfaction of an emotional display. *Two can play that game, lady.*

I desperately want a drink of water but am still on thickened liquids and unable to swallow any regular liquid, like water. To be told I will never again drive, never finish my college degree, never learn anything new for the rest of my life, or improve much more in any capacity, if at all, is crushing. It is almost physically painful.

Just a few months ago, I was a college senior with a promising future. I had been in the best shape of my life, headed for what I believed would be a terrific career and a quality life. All my life's efforts and time up to that point had been spent with getting a superior education, which would allow me to have a stellar job and would naturally lead to other good things—a family, a house filled with kids' voices... adventures and dreams my young mind was only beginning to wrap itself around. Being only eight weeks away from completing one of my long-dreamed-about ambitions meant that another step was remarkably close to completion, and life's goals were that much closer.

What is my future now? Was it life in a wheelchair, drinking thickened liquids, and being cared for like an invalid? My entire life had been spent preparing for and looking forward to the future. A promising future of success and impacting lives. I had just been informed my future would be bleak and insignificant.

Momentarily, I think back to when I looked at the final grade that I had received in the community college class I took during high school—I had passed and that meant one less class I'd have to take and pay for in college. Saving time and money was huge and absolutely vital in my world. I remember looking at my final grades in classes like Physics, Calculus, or Organic Chemistry at Bluffton. Once I knew I had passed them, I did a little dance. After hearing these words in this meeting, the dancing and all those feelings of accomplishment became irrelevant. Those long hours of reading and figuring everything out, all the studying and cramming, were rendered worthless.

Further pain came from the unsettling realization that thousands of hours of athletic practices, lifting weights, running, and taking care of my physical health all became meaningless.

All the struggles, sacrifices, and efforts in virtually every aspect of my life, immediately turned to nothing. Nothing but a waste of time.

As I sat there in shock, I grew smaller, my shoulders caving in, and my chin came to rest on my chest. I had just been decked with a sucker punch to my confidence. I had not seen her punch coming or seen her as a thief, but she had just stolen my recovery spirit. All of life's dreams had just been demolished. I was jolted from my thoughts when the doctor who had given me the test told us, "We're all done here."

I remember thinking, *What does she mean, "all done?" All done with the tests? The evaluations? Further treatment?*

Something positive from this neuropsychological test results meeting sneaks into my mind; early on this callous individual had told me physical activity is the number one healer for the brain. Okay, that I could relate to. Physical activity had been a huge part of my life. Though, it was surprising she was the one telling me to get physical activity.

I was daunted by her verdict, especially since I was in a wheelchair being told I will never get out and the mention that brain injuries heal the most within the first six months, with little progress after those six months. My injury occurred at the beginning of March, and this is October. Was I "all done" with the rest of my life?

As my mother wheeled me out of the room, her movements were no longer steady. I felt the shakiness in her steps as she pushed me along. She took me to my therapy appointment and, as usual, helped as much as she could to get me set up. As she is assisting me to the mat, I gaze at her with hopeless eyes saying, "I went to school for nothing." After getting me settled, Mom excused herself, something she had never done before.

Mom said later she did not want to let me see her so distraught, as it might have upset me even more. To avoid crying in front of me, she walked through the lobby out into the hallway, where she began to sob. Almost as if in solidarity, torrential rain poured over the large windows in the hallway. Mom stood there alone, looking out and thinking, *maybe this is a wakeup call. Maybe we were being too optimistic. They were just trying to be helpful and realistic.*

She observed some college students rushing through the soaking rain on the campus of this teaching hospital. Her heart was breaking as she told herself her son would never run through a college campus... would never run at all again, and she completely broke down.

In that moment, for the first time since the accident, Mom had no hope.

It lay dead on that office floor.

Once she got her emotions under control, she returned to the rehab gym. A resident rehab doctor walked by and asked Mom how she was doing. She softly replied, "Not so good."

He asked for details, and Mom explained about the appointment. The resident doctor stepped closer, looked her straight in the eye, and, weighing each word, sternly said, "Prove them wrong, Karen. *Prove them wrong.*"

Mom remembers the fiery demeanor of that doctor to this day. He really meant what he said. I did have much further to go yet, but nobody knew at the time how far I could go, not even me. The one positive thing I learned from the evaluation meeting was the number one healer for the brain is physical activity. I told myself, *okay, I can do that.*

I had been a trained athlete and no stranger to strenuous activity. If pushing the limits of my physical abilities was what

130

it took, I was going to do everything in my power to make it happen.

———

7th Inning Stretch

I thought the journal entries below, and the emotions surrounding them, would be useful to the reader's understanding of my healing process, as well as the impact on my entire family. I included some of my mother's journal entries while I was in inpatient care at The University of Toledo Medical Center (UTMC).

These are recorded entries as they appeared. No content has been added but some content with specific names has been left out for the privacy of those individuals. Punctuation has been added to a couple journal entries to make reading easier and a few explanations have been inserted in parenthesis for privacy reasons or for better understanding.

April 15, 2007 *(day after I arrived at UTMC from Atlanta)*
Lots of evaluations by doctors and therapists.

4-16
Six sessions of therapy today. Speech, occupational, and physical.

4-18
Brushed teeth on his own—along sides and up and down in

front—got tired left toothbrush in mouth while resting a minute then resumed brushing.

Fitted for helmet.

Rob's FMLA (Family and Medical Leave Act) denied second time.

4-19

Went for swallow test. Aspirated some pudding, so Tim will have to repeat the swallow test in one to two weeks. Received helmet today—waved goodbye to speech therapist (for first time) and making more throat noises. Trisha buys stickers for Tim's helmet—sports, Muppets, and Army. She plays balloon catch with Tim in the gym.

4-20

Cast removed—ankle bending more--recast to stretch even more than before. (Friends from Bluffton) came—guys cut Tim's hair! Then he gets shower—has very restful night.

4-21

Tim is so tired after AM therapy he fell asleep with helmet on!

4-23

Tim's left ankle recast.

4-24

Wrote Trisha and Tonya's names and Tigger (family dog) plus a message to Mom and Dad. "Help me", and another word or two we aren't sure about. Helped dress himself and brushed his teeth.

4-26

Tim had cast on left ankle. Cast removed again, and received Botox shots in left arm and left leg muscles. Pointed to different muscles on his body-abs-pecs-biceps.

4-27

Received balloons from Ida teachers (high school).

4-30

Left ankle recast. Began to use wound vac for bed sore.

5-1

Cousin spending the night. Went outside for physical Therapy—Tim put his bare right foot in the grass.

5-3

125.5 lb. Thursdays are now weighing days.

5-4

Numbed nose with spray and put tube with a camera on the end down Tim's nose. Has ulcer on bottom of left vocal cord impacting the voice box. (will take) eight weeks to heal.

5-5

Uncle Troy and Aunt Kay spent day with Tim. Rob and I went to Tonya's softball tournament at Jefferson.

5-6

Trisha watched Tim all day so Rob and I could go to Bluffton's baccalaureate and graduation. We (received) an empty diploma for Tim.

5-10

Tim shaves with electric razor for the first time. Had cast put on left arm.

5-13

Tim prints me a Mother's Day card! (An Ida friend) figures out the words on Mother's Day card. "Little did I realize how lucky I am to share each day with you." At 10:30, Tim is agitated again with his mouth. He writes "stupid gum" and keeps trying to pick out a wad of gum in his mouth. Hits self in head but stops immediately when I talk soothingly to him. Used a pen light, can't see anything in his mouth.

5-15

Tim says first word, "Ouch", during recasting of his left arm.

5-16

(An Ida friend) comes to be with Tim so Rob and I can go to Tonya's double header in Onsted.

5-18

Aunt Lucy stays with Tim so Rob and I can go to Tonya's double header at Tecumseh. Tim laughs with Aunt Lucy at funniest home videos show.

5-19

Trisha stays with Tim while we go to Ida's JV softball tournament.

5-20

Uncle Troy and Aunt Kay with Tim so we can do things at home.

5-21

Tim talks a lot. Mom, Dad, hi, bye, I love you, Happy Mom's Day, Red Lobster, Go Blue.

(Tim's) Story aired on Channel 11. "The Will to Survive" at 11 p.m. about the accident and his recovery so far.

5-26

Uncle Troy and Aunt Kay spend the day with Tim. Rob and I go to (Tonya's) varsity Adrian tournament.

5-29

Cousin Ruth spends the night. Tim sees social worker for 1st time. Very receptive. Rob and I go to Blissfield to watch Tonya in varsity pre-Districts—Tonya gets first varsity hit (single).

5-30

Tim pets Rob's beard and strokes his cheek, hugs him, and says, I love you. Pulls me to his chest hugs me and says, I love you. Then writes, I love both of you. Plays catch with an elderly gentleman in PT with a balloon. Tim bops the guy in the forehead with the balloon. Tim laughs and laughs with his head back. I took a picture on my cell phone.

6-1

Maternal uncle and aunt bring Tim's maternal grandma and grandpa for a visit, plus friends from Ida and Bluffton's football coach and his wife come. Tim is nervous about tomorrow's surgery and writes he's scared. Walked 1/3 mile on the treadmill—practiced stepping on a wood platform about 10 inches high. Played war in speech and won.

6-2

The surgeon does the surgery to put the piece of Tim's skull (we brought from Atlanta) back in. Surgery was 2 hours. 11:10 a.m.-1:10 p.m. Tim no more helmet! Was not intubated (tube down throat) in the normal way because of the potential to damage the healing of the ulcer on his left vocal cord from being intubated in Atlanta. They used microscope and could see some of the healing on his vocal cord had progressed to a callus. Spent night in surgery ICU. Sounds (of the ICU) brought back bad memories for Rob and I. Day nurse very good and also had another for afternoon and a night nurse I couldn't remember name taking vitals every hour. Tim had a foley and same monitor as in Grady for blood pressure, heart rate, resp. IV.

6-3

Tim moved up to 5th floor. Face swelling on left side and left eye. Doctor said this is a good sign and would worry if there was no swelling. (nurse from rehab floor) comes down and changes wound vac dressing.

6-4

Tim moved up to rehab 6th floor about 5:30. Good to be back. Left eye now swollen shut.

6-5

(Inpatient physical therapist) says Tim has thrush (fungus) on tongue (and) on roof of mouth. Begin brushing medicine on it to kill. Wound vac is removed! Go to a wet/dry dressing. Swelling going down. Very tired today and dizzy.

6-6

(Friends from Ida and Bluffton) come for a visit. Rob and I go get our hair cut and come back to spend the night. Shoots everyone (with) suction cup dart gun a friend bought him. It is

baseball day on unit. Tim wears Tigers shirt and Michigan cap. Hits ball off tee (indoor plastic bat) he works to place his own left hand on bat. Plays balloon volleyball with other patients & spikes many times.

6-8

I'm helping Tim with drinking thickened Gatorade while he sits on the side of his bed when he hits the mattress with his fist and is very frustrated. He indicates he's frustrated with not being able to swallow and close his lips then he begins to cry, then sob about his body. I put my arm around his shoulder and we discuss the accident. I get out the footprints poem from his room and read to him and he nods and cries. Indicates he wants to write. Writes, "I love God" and I say, "God loves you too and he's helping us." Tim writes, "I love God and I pray nightly to Jesus." I explain about (another brain injury patient) from Atlanta. (suffered a) TBI (after being hit with 70 mph ball during a game) and read Tim the framed poem (that patient) gave him. Rob comes in (and) sits on other side of Tim and we hug and talk and cry. After about 30-40 minutes, Tim wants to lie down and he falls asleep until dinner. He is sad and quiet the rest of the afternoon. (Friends from Ida) come in the evening and Tim has improved in his mood & laughs some. Shoots with his dart gun at a small Mickey Mouse doll a nurse found.

6-9

Uncle Troy and Aunt Kay come to spend the day with Tim. Bring him Ivan Rodriguez framed signed jersey. Tim is elated!

6-10

Tim writes *if anyone else (of our family) was in the accident. We say no. That it was the Bluffton baseball team on the way to Florida. We ask if he remembers being on the bus, shakes his head no. Tim writes, "Was I hurt the worst?"*

Rob and I look at each other and agree it's okay to tell Tim about the deaths. I ask Tim if I can hold his hand, and he puts his right in mine and I begin to cry and say, "No, Tim, no, you weren't the worst. Some boys died, Tim. Do you remember the (bus driver and his wife)? They died too, Tim."

He points to the letters and spells "wow."

I ask him if he wants to know the names of the boys that died. He nods. (tell Tim one name). "Do you remember?" Shakes his head no. Rob describes him and Tim remembers and nods. Tim is shocked at another name.

"I know, Tim, I know. And (another name). Tim, do you remember him?" Shakes his head no. "Tim (another name) died, too. Do you remember him?" He nods and spells "wow."

We show him the picture in the scrapbook of the pictures of the five boys and (the bus driver & his wife.) I say, "It was an accident, Tim. The bus crashed. (The bus driver) thought he was still on I-75."

He spells "wow."

"They're in heaven now with God looking down on us, helping us."

Tim writes, "That is good they're in heaven."

I say, "Yes, Tim, that is good. We have an awesome God."

He nods and points upward.

"Many people are praying for you, Tim, for us as a family. The crash happened in Atlanta, Georgia. (Your cousins) came to the hospital (to help).

6-12

Tim has another swallow study. He writes beforehand, "I need to study for the swallow test." He aspirates the thin liquid —a small amount—but doesn't even cough. (Inpatient speech pathologist) is with us. Tim is very disappointed. Pounds himself in the leg with fist. Writes, "I'm sorry. I wanted a second chance to try it." Puts his fingers to his head like a gun.

His next session with (social worker) so we tell her ahead of time and she meets with Tim. He feels a little better after the session. He throws a stress ball against the wall before his next session. Rob fires some himself at the door. Nurse comes to check if we're okay.

I kneel to his level and say, "Don't be sorry. It's not your fault." Rob is at his side saying encouraging things. Rob begins to cry. We feel so bad because Tim feels so bad. Rob cries in the bathroom during Tim's session with (social worker). Too upset to talk. (Friends from Ida and Bluffton roommate) come for a visit. (Friend from Ida) brings Tim chocolate cheesecake. Tim laughs and is doing a little better.

6-14

When I get to the hospital Rob is very excited because Tim said "flag day" so clearly. Paternal uncle, aunt, Grandma Berta, other aunt, and Trisha come at 2 p.m. to see Tim in some of his therapies. One aunt stays with Tim while the rest of us go to get (fast-food.) (Social worker) tells us today that she allowed Tim to express his anger with the stress ball, but they then discussed were there other times in his life before the accident he felt frustrated and he writes, "sports." She asked what he did. Did he give up and he said no, and she used that to keep him determined to keep trying. Tim begins to communicate much more than before. Speech and writing getting clearer. (Resident doctor) removes (head) stitches—wound healing nicely.

6-15

(Ida friends) come for a visit, bring flowers from their home. (Bluffton football coach) and wife come and ask us to keep September 1 open. 1st football game—bring Tim a Bible.

6-16

Tim has speech and (physical therapy) (with) two of the therapists he'll have in outpatient therapy. Bluffton roommate's family comes for a visit.

6-17

Father's Day—Tim writes card for Rob. "Dad (partner) there are so many ways I'm blessed and you are special. Love, Tim." Also another page: "I work my butt off so I can come home with you. I love you!" (A friend from Ida) comes for visit. Hasn't seen Tim in a month. Amazed at changes. Tim kicks butt on (rehab gym) machine with only left arm and leg. Trisha and Tonya come.

6-18

(Social worker) brings us lunch again. We practice transfer from wheelchair to silver van front seat and practice closing chair for transport. (Employee from a home care company) is coming to meet us to see which nurse would be good for us. Tim walks from gym to elevator with (inpatient physical therapists) help. Rides down to lobby (and) walks across lobby to bench outside. Rob pulls up van and (inpatient physical therapist) transfers Tim with chair to passenger seat of van. Then Rob did it, then I. (inpatient physical therapist) also shows us how to fold up (wheelchair) for today.

6-19

Speech is even more improved. He went to the ear, nose, and throat doctor. Last visit 5-4-07. Numbed Tim's nose again & put down tube with camera on the end. Ulcer is healed. Tim says ahhh and eeee. No permanent damage to the vocal cords.

Doctor says speech will continue to improve and be better in six months to a year. "The brain is building new railroad tracks & your voice will be fine in time." (An inpatient speech pathologist) thinks because of the huge strides Tim's made in the last six days the time frame may be three to six months.

Bottom of the 7th
Personal Reflections

Yes, I had been waiting for the day I would finally go home, but I often did not even think about it, simply because I did not have the mental space to. I desperately wanted to get out of the terrible hospital but was too busy being angry or worn-out or hungry or anything else that I felt in the moment to truly focus on the fact that I would one day leave.

Then, what I had anticipated as an easy, joyful day without rehab and the ultimate prize of leaving this inpatient hospital nightmare, instead turned into a challenging unpleasant day. A day requiring more effort than expected. A day I realized some hard truths. A day when difficult-to-hear, unexpected facts were learned. It was not all bad though.

It was certainly uplifting to see the "WELCOME HOME" sign from my sisters once I was rolled up the ramp and came in the front door. Seeing that sign gave me a special, magical feeling and my sisters may never fully realize the mental boost they provided. I felt welcomed and loved. Though my therapists and hospital staff did what they could and often went above and beyond, there was not much in terms of a feeling of welcome in the overall scenario of inpatient rehabilitation. Trisha and Tonya both get MVP for the day I finally got to come home.

What was encouraging as well was the ample outpouring of

love from the neighborhood, friends, and even complete strangers. Along with my family, colleagues, and various members of society all certainly stepped up to the plate. People from Ida, Bluffton, and Toledo came to the house to visit. I soon learned about kindnesses extended to me and my family.

Around that time, I learned about the fundraiser in Ida and Lourdes University offering me the full-ride scholarship. Some friends who had included their own page in my scrapbook pitched in and bought me a game system, and other well-wishers brought food. I heard others held a softball game fundraiser, with all of them wearing "Berta All Stars" t-shirts. Every t-shirt had the number 15 on the back—this was my uniform number when playing college baseball.

I learned of a couple Bluffton classmates who ran a pasta-dinner fundraiser, with at least one waitress from the Findlay Fricker's donating her tips and others offering to help in ways they knew how. Frequently, we could use the help, and hope-fully all of you know it was greatly appreciated. One of my biology professors from Bluffton even brought an aloe plant when he came to visit my home in Michigan. The Aloe plant is known to help with healing. Fitting, don't you think? God has blessed me tremendously over my lifetime with great colleagues and friends.

Throughout my life, I've always been a big eater. Coming home also had me looking forward to being able to eat real food. To my complete dismay, any food I ate still had to be puréed, or blended. Talk about a major letdown. Somehow, however, when my mom prepared puréed food, it tasted much better than hospital food. Mom gets MVP for preparing my food, even if it had to be puréed.

The "only you can fix it" conversation with Dad was not easy to digest, but I really needed to hear it. Dad was on my team and was working his tail off to give me the best chance at recovery. Yes, I made the choice to keep fighting, but Dad encouraged me and was there for me. For that conversation, and for fighting to reduce the number of medications I had to take, Dad was MVP. If you're an MVP of any team, you first must get the proper instruction.

I was shocked when I learned that some of my UTMC therapists had been learning rehabilitation techniques at the Shepherd center in Atlanta at the time of the accident. The Shepard rehab center is known for their first-class rehab care. Therapists at UTMC had brought that instruction and knowledge back and were using it in my rehab. Knowing Atlanta had wanted me to get rehab from Shepherd, this was another unique element on my side.

I am still amazed at the many mysterious ways in which the Lord works. I couldn't have thought that out any better. Talk about divine intervention. God was on my team again. It is incredibly uplifting to know God was a part of my support network and had my back.

Speaking of assistance, I cannot imagine it was a pleasant experience to be a family member of mine during this whole trial. My sister, Tonya, was willing to help me, and, unfortunately, it meant getting vomited on. I am truly grateful for her help on that disastrous morning that turned out okay largely because of her efforts.

Just as each player has a specific skill for their position on the baseball field, each of my family members played their own unique role in my road to recovery. Tonya probably would not have volunteered to be the one puked on had she known in advance what was to transpire, but that was the place she was put in. I mean, usually you get to select your own spot, but she got stuck with that one. Tonya, I am sorry—I know that was not a fun position. But if it makes you feel better, you win MVP for that day.

There were moments of fun in the outpatient rehabilitation gym, and they stand out to me to this day. One was the guy yelling at me about the trachea scar. It wasn't until a while after that incident that I learned he also had a brain injury, but again, his variety might have caused him to lose his social filter. I thank the Lord, I did not lose mine because who knows what I would have said in response to his yelling about my trachea scar, and it could have been an ugly scene. Instead, that moment was turned into what my mom and I have tons of fun reliving and retelling, always with a lot of compassion for the man with the brain injury.

A day or two before that event, an old friend that I had played football with and graduated from Ida with came to visit. He brought his girlfriend too. He had also suffered a brain injury from a car accident that resulted in a trach scar in his neck. His girlfriend had told me women think trach scars are sexy, so I had that fresh in my head. There are moments of great timing, and this certainly was one. Huh, it appears that was something new I learned.

Another funny instance from outpatient comes to mind— when a physical therapist assistant was putting my leg brace back on while I was still using the wheelchair. She was kneeling in front of me. I got the mischievous idea to put one foot on each of her shoulders. It just seemed like a good place to put my feet up! Another great timing moment. That lasted only a few seconds though, before she swatted them off with a laugh and a smile.

Not everything was fun, though. There were plenty of despairing moments.

Shortly after I came home from the hospital but before Mike and Molly's wedding that September, I was sitting in my wheelchair at home, seated right in front of our family's living room window. As I observed outside, it was a beautiful sunny day. The first thought that came to me in that moment was, *I am extremely happy for Mike and Molly—they deserve a life full of happiness and fulfillment.*

Other thoughts, however, were telling me, *Obviously I'm not good enough for what they have. I must not have worked hard enough or done things correctly. Here I am, stuck inside in a wheelchair on this beautiful sunny day and life is passing me by. Mike and Molly are getting married, preparing for the biggest day of their lives, and here I am, the same age as them, yet sitting in a wheelchair inside my parents' house, unable to wipe my own rear end and occasionally drooling—a long way from marriage. What did I do to deserve this?*

Talk about feeling defeated.

Yes, I am fighting to honor my teammates killed, and yes, I am fighting to earn back some aspects of my life. I am grateful to God I can fight for what I am able to earn back, but still those negative thoughts come on occasion. I am only human.

Weddings are events charged with positive energy—truly beautiful times—especially when you're asked to be in them. It is quite an honor to be asked to participate in somebody's wedding, and I don't take that lightly.

By the time of the wedding, almost seven months after the accident, the bus crash had become national news. Most people who would be present would know me and would understand that I had experienced some significant difficulties during my recovery and wasn't exactly myself again. I was still using my wheelchair and had not been standing a whole lot yet. That is why I made it a point not to stand until everyone was facing Molly. They are both wonderful and giving friends to this day.

In fact, early on after the accident, Mike made a Tim Berta profile page on the Caringbridge website. He wrote outstanding things about me, and I want him to know how much they mean. I vaguely remember some of these talks but doubt I would have on my own had he not written about them.

One thing he shared was that he had told me, during our freshman year at Bluffton, that he wished he was bigger, stronger, and faster on the football field. I responded, "Well, try to be grateful for the opportunity given to us, to continue our playing careers. Most people in high school we played with don't have this chance. As hard as it may be, try to look at the bright side of attending college and still being able to play football."

He remembers this conversation, and that means the world to me. It was another human moment and boosted my spirits.

Deep tissue massage was also immensely helpful. I wish I could put into words what that unbelievably kind gesture means and the amount of good it did. Certainly, it helped physically but also mentally and emotionally from just chatting with the caring local massage therapist at a time when I needed a boost.

In the days after the neuropsychological examination result meeting, my self-esteem was at its lowest. Over the course of a couple weeks, I remember a thought like this- *"If the life I must look forward to is really what they told me based on those test results, then why didn't I just die.* So, I was feeling sorry for myself. *What kind of "good plan" for me is this God?* Still more deep thought over that time span brought thoughts of Zach, David, Scott, Cody and Tyler who were killed. Then I knew what I needed to do. *Regardless of what my life brings, honoring them is my life's purpose."* I needed special moments and memories of people like Mike and the skilled massage therapist to help raise my spirits and hopes. What also aided my mentality was the memory of the bridesmaids dancing around me at the wedding. In case you're curious, at the end of the book there is a link to my website with photos of the wedding along with what Mike wrote on CaringBridge.

Those memories and feelings were like a drink of cold water just when you need it after a workout. As a former college athlete physical activity had been a huge part of my life, and I saw no reason to stop now. The anger from the neuro-psych evaluation and fury from not being able to do certain tasks on my own really drove me.

I had made up my mind. I was determined. I was going to do everything in my power to exercise and stay in shape. Exercising when I had the chance would honor my deceased teammates. Tenaciously fighting for more improvements when science told me I would not improve anymore would pay tribute to them. Honoring my deceased teammates was bigger than myself, and that served to give meaning to my life, even though it was now far from the life I had planned.

At the end of the day, I also praise the Lord that I can walk at all and that my physical therapists put in extra effort on my behalf. Taking the foot braces on and off was not an easy or quick process, even in outpatient. I am grateful to God for "those people" that I, in much of that early on confusing and bewildering time, mistakenly perceived as my enemies and tormentors. They were the ones encouraging me all along. An outpatient physical therapist told me the only way you're going to get more fluid and improve walking is by doing it.

To this day one of my favorite exercises is just a simple walk. I do my best to honor my fallen teammates with every step I take.

8TH INNING

Top of the 8th
Visit to the Mound
October 2007 - May 2009

When Mom and I got home after the neuropsychological test results meeting at UTMC, we were alone in the house. She was transferring me from the wheelchair to my bed. She was crying. I felt angry that they had made my mother cry. I told her I was sorry.

With rage, I fumed, "Nobody tells me what I can and cannot do! I can't go very fast, but I can move forward. I don't care what their stats say. Their stats don't consider what happens when God and I get together."

Mom began to sob and finally announced that we were going to have a family meeting.

Later that evening, all five of us sat around our kitchen table. Mom and I fully explained why we were greatly upset, what had happened, and how we were treated. We explained how we'd been told, according to the test results, that I may retain different things I had learned from before, but I'd never learn anything new the rest of my life.

Upon hearing this, Trisha began to shake her head in protest. "But that… No… But that's just not true. He *can* learn new things. He just did the other night!" She then rattled off different moments where I *had* learned new things since after the accident.

Something I had come to know after my return home is that two of Trisha's friends—ones I had not met before the bus crash—had been especially helpful while I was in the hospital. They would answer the front door when any media arrived at the house. Since at first only Mom and Dad had gone to Atlanta, the media would often show up at our home, constantly bugging Trisha, or Tonya. Those two enormous guys would answer the door and tell whoever was standing there that Trisha and Tonya were not home. Trisha had talked about that to me, and I remembered her telling that story.

Trisha believed in me and made that clear during our family meeting. She was correct—I had learned new things and was doing so consistently. But these people who had given me the test and results were educated in this field. They each had earned through years of study a PhD. This was their area of expertise, not ours. They had probably seen hundreds if not thousands of patients with damaged brains.

We certainly had our doubts. Were we just idealistically and irrationally optimistic? Were we just fooling ourselves? Because they were not people on my medical team, and therefore more "objective," had they been designated to make my family face reality?

However, Trisha had cracked their wall of education with her facts—her real-life examples of my progress. During one part of the discussion, Tonya stood and slammed her fist down on the table. "No!" she roared. "We are Bertas! We do *not* give up!"

And that was our rally cry. We made our choice. I would keep fighting for as long as I could. It was what I could do to pay tribute to teammates who did not have the gift of that choice. It was what I could do to show respect for my family, and it was what I could do to honor myself and the gift of survival that I had been given.

Together we would ride this journey out as far as it would take us, however far that might be. Tonya had captured our roots, our very family core. We weren't discouraged anymore —we were determined.

Of course, this did not mean everything would be much easier. And the battle I fought at home in terms of speech therapy was a perfect example. My voice had not been used for months after the accident. My speech was jumbled and slurred. Yes, I spoke a word here and there, but my voice was not nearly where it should be. I needed to relearn how to use my breath while talking, how to pronounce different words, forming the sounds with my now weak tongue. If I didn't have to talk, usually I wouldn't, which didn't help things.

Aunt Lucy is a former teacher of hearing-impaired students. Her whole career dealt with methods of speaking more under-standably. Her daughter, my cousin, is a registered speech pathologist. Both my aunt and cousin had graciously volun-teered to come to my house weekly for extra speech work. They chose a day that worked for me when I wasn't going to UTMC.

You would think I would have been on board with this. I was in outpatient rehab and had a better understanding of what was going on. You would assume that, if I always wanted to go the extra mile, I would be perfectly willing to go right along with something that would help me improve a lost skill vital to flourishing in the future.

For some reason, this was not the case. The longer time

dragged on, the more it felt like sinking quicksand. My air was starting to get cut off and I was becoming desperate to breathe. Lately this feeling was synonymous for my entire life and future.

I made a choice that I didn't want to do extra speech anymore, and I became irritable and impatient. I'm not sure if I was rude per say but certainly was at my breaking point. Maybe it was because it was more therapy work at a time when I was not scheduled for any. Maybe it was because I was lazy and wanted to relax on my days off. I think mostly it was that I didn't think it was necessary and I was unbelievably rundown with all the therapies being "inflicted" upon me. I probably figured, *Why do I need more speech therapy? I know what I'm trying to say. I sound fine. Why can't people understand me?*

After a couple months of these out of therapy voice sessions, I started to complain or groan about doing the additional speech work to whomever would listen. I was already doing extra stretches with my left arm and trying to relearn how to tie my shoes with my new stiff and barely usable left fingers and hand. All this while I was home on my days off. I told myself I didn't want to do anything else on top of the hard work I was already doing.

One day, my cousin, Ruth, talked to my mom and said, "Please intervene and talk to him. You're his parents, and he'll forget and forgive you a lot quicker." She was worried lecturing me would only make me resent the therapy more.

My mom did what she could in terms of encouraging me and desperately tried to get me to understand my speech needed lots of work. With the mind of an adolescent and from my limited perspective, my mom didn't know anything. I usually stuck with it and went along with their speech exercises, but certainly had my days of not wanting to do the extra work, especially as time wore on.

Soon, I compromised and had the idea of reading them a book.

Ruth agreed. "Sure, we can do that."

I did not make it clear that would be the end goal but did assume stopping, once I finished reading the book, was the obvious and clear path. That way there would be a certain and discernible ending point. It took about a month but after I finished reading *To Kill a Mockingbird*, I thought I was done.

When Mom, Dad, Ruth and Aunt Lucy decided they were going to continue visiting, I became despondent again, thinking, *I even read a whole book out loud, and I'm still not good enough.* It felt once more that my best was not good enough. There seemed to be no finish line.

They were family members willing to put in extra time with no reward, so why was I not cooperative? If I was trying to honor my fallen teammates who did not have a choice and I always wanted to go the extra step, why was I resisting? I just don't have a good answer for that, other than being human, and imperfect. My frustration often got the better of me.

———

About a month after the one-year anniversary of the accident, I began to get headaches. The headaches were not debilitating but they were noticeably unpleasant. At times each day, it felt like there was a small object the size of a pencil boring into my skull.

X-rays determined my body had rejected my original skull piece and a second surgery needed to be performed. What was used to substitute for my skull piece was the material they use to replace hips. That said, I'm a little disappointed I do not set off metal detectors. No titanium for me.

After the surgery, I saw the brain surgeon for a follow-up. He said that he believed God had worked a miracle through me and suggested I share my story, especially with students. He reported that people will not listen to him and, as I was leaving, in a matter-of-fact tone, stated, "People will listen to you. You have a pretty face."

After hearing this, I stopped and slowly turned around, kind of chuckling. I had no idea what to think. He was a foreign doctor. He may not have known "pretty" in our culture is not often used to describe males. Or, he may have known exactly what he was saying and was joking. Either way, looking back, it makes me laugh and I'm flattered. Still feeling worthless and undesirable even after I was not using the wheelchair anymore, this small instance gave me a tiny victory as I walked out of that office.

It wasn't that I decided to walk one day and simply got out of the wheelchair. Just like other things in my recovery, it was a slow process. I had to relearn what I used to take for granted. The act of walking was now a chore and required much thought, concentration, and focus.

In inpatient rehab, my dedicated physical therapists had done serial casting not only on my left arm but also on my left foot. Once this casting aligned my left foot to the point of being able to function in a walk, I began the tedious process of learning. The final goal was to keep my balance while walking independently, without parallel bars or side rails or the consistent speed of a treadmill. "Real world" walking.

When I was exercising off the treadmill, the outpatient therapists started me walking with a walker. Then there were months of using that walker along with additional practice on treadmills and between balance bars. When I began exercising off the treadmill, I graduated to a four-pronged cane. Afterwards, a single leg cane, then no cane. It was also a progression once I began to walk without any cane. There would be days where I said, "I am just too tired to walk at all today."

We still had the wheelchair and would use it except for my

physical therapy sessions. There were other days when I would attempt to walk slowly. If there was a wall or chairs or tables or anything available to support my balance, I would use those to lean on while maneuvering. If there was nothing available, I would take one step, gather myself, then take another step, gather myself, then take another step, and so on.

I was a former college athlete, wide receiver in football, and often used as a pinch runner and base stealer in baseball. I was used to going places quickly, and moving fluidly, and currently there was nothing quick or fluid about my new way of walking.

Out of the familiar confines and set speeds of the treadmill, my left leg had no single leg balance or general coordination. In addition to this issue, my muscles would not function as they used to. My left calf or my left knee occasionally locked. This was another moment I felt victory and defeat at the same time —victory because again by the grace of God, using the wheelchair was no longer a necessity. Defeat because walking was now strenuous and challenging.

———

There was a smaller gym we would sometimes use to exercise. This gym had a track, and the therapist knew how many laps equaled a mile. After learning this equivalency, the competitive fire rose inside—I told my therapist that I wanted to see if I could go a full mile. At least in this scenario there would be a set objective and discernable conclusion. Obvious goals and perceptible ending targets had been my life until the accident. There was no visible goal or stopping point that I could see while in rehabilitation and that aspect drove me insane. Going after this mile walk was comforting and gave me back a piece of who I had been—a part of the "old Tim."

Since Mom had driven me to therapy that day, I began with

her standing in the middle of the track. The therapist walked beside me in case I tripped or became too fatigued to continue. It was a fight. I did get weary and shaky. I wanted to call it off more than once. The fighter-achiever mentality that had been killed in the neuro-psych evaluation and then resurrected in our family meeting emerged. I kept my eye on the goal and kept moving forward.

It took the whole hour, but I walked all sixteen laps, one step at a time. On the last lap, my mom stood at the finish line, and I collapsed into her hug with another huge victory under my belt.

After accomplishing this gargantuan task, I printed off a sign reading, "On May 16th, 2008, I, Tim Berta, walked a mile!! I'm STILL improving!" I taped it on the office door of the social worker.

In counseling, we had talked about not obsessing on what I could do before and now couldn't, but to keep all focus on improvements, tiny or large. Again, trying to find all the joy possible. Walking that mile was a huge achievement and showed I was improving.

Of course, a bonus was the social worker's office was right next to the office of "those PhD's." Briefly, I considered taping the note onto their door. It would be justified vengeance. I wasn't supposed to improve from that day of the evaluation, and I had. I was walking, one of the things they said I'd never do. I also considered giving into my competitive spirit and *walking* into the doctor's office. I imagined looking her in the eye and slamming my piece of paper onto her desk. And then I would yell, "It's seven months after your eval. I'm STILL GOING! I'm STILL IMPROVING! Put THAT in your stats!"

The more I thought that through though, I realized, if I were to do that, I would be lowering myself. I would be using my energy for anger. I needed every ounce of my energy to prove their test evaluation was completely wrong. To myself, not them. Their test findings meant nothing to me. I was truly beginning to hold my life to a higher standard. I had big goals I still wanted to achieve and no time for bitterness.

———

In the year following the accident a few weeks before summer season officially began, I went for another swallow test. This time, I was not wheeled but walked into what I recognized as the same room where I passed the swallow test to be able to eat solid food. Huh, there's something else new I learned.

On this day, however, the test would be for thin liquids, specifically. After entering, a remarkable calm came over me. By no means did this indicate I didn't care about passing this thin-liquid portion of another swallow test. I wanted this so badly that nerves had already started once I walked in, but I also had confidence that passing this was a done deal. I felt prepared and up for the challenge. I had been attacking this problem for a while and was going to use a couple tactics.

One strategy came from an occupational therapist. I would be sitting with excellent posture and while I swallowed the water, I would tuck my chin to my chest. I had also been working on the strength in my neck with my cousin, Ruth, at home in speech. Attempting to strengthen my throat muscles so I could drink water certainly gave me a goal with a discernable end point.

As I was handed the cup of water, I looked down for a second, almost willing it to go to my stomach and not my lungs. I slowly took a drink. Just as before, there was no reaction from me resulting in a cough. I fleetingly considered pretending to cough but didn't, just anxiously sat there with my eyes darting around the room searching for any type of hint.

The doctor then asked me to take another swallow of water. I did the same procedure again and swallowed the water. Just as before, there was no reaction or cough. Unlike the previous test a few months ago, there was no reaction because every ounce of liquid went into my stomach, right where it should. The doctor then announced the results here would be the same as with any other healthy human.

I had passed!

Try to imagine a time when you were the thirstiest you have ever been and what it felt like when you were finally able to have a drink. It was the true feeling of being refreshed. It was also the sweet taste of victory. All the anger, sourness, feelings of being attacked, and heartbreak temporarily went away after learning I could, once again, drink water.

In that moment of learning I could drink thin liquids, those feelings vanished down the drain. Pun intended. I had yet another monumental victory.

I requested Red Lobster again to celebrate. Nothing quenches your thirst like water, especially when you have gone without it for over a year.

———

As going to rehab three days a week continued, a new problem soon emerged. Each time I tried to eat or drink anything, it wouldn't go into my lungs or my stomach—it went right into my lap. My right arm and hand would begin to actively shake as I would attempt to eat, drink, or write as I used to. My left arm was useless and now my right arm was shaking.

I felt angry and hopeless again. It seemed like I was taking two steps forward in my recovery, then one or even two steps back. Sulking, I told myself, *now that it's real food and liquid, I can't even enjoy it.* Yet another confounding time in my recovery.

We scheduled an appointment with a neurologist who happened to be at UTMC, named Doctor Relm. He was so popular it would be several months before he had an opening. Once in the appointment, we explained my good right arm was no longer steady while performing everyday tasks, and that it would start shaking practically out of nowhere. My family and I were scared. We worried the tremor might gradually spread to the rest of my body.

He had me reach out my hand, bring it in and touch my nose. My arm and fingers were uncontrollably shaking as I attempted this and could not accomplish that simple task. The entire Berta family was petrified at what could be happening.

However, I will never forget my shock after hearing what the neurologist said. He looked at me and calmly stated, "Well, Tim, this is a good sign. What it does is tell me your brain is still healing. I'm not a betting man, but if I were, I'd bet that, given a year, your tremor will be better, if not totally gone."

At this point, I was thinking, *Huh? What kind of a quack is this guy? Here I wait months to see him, and he is not going to offer me any treatment, just tell me to wait? What gives?*

———

In the twelve-month time frame between that appointment with Doctor Relm and the next one, Dad and I had a meeting. This meeting was with both of my two remaining biology professors at Bluffton, one of my courses being in Developmental Biology, and the other in Microbiology.

Once I began to complete my work for Bluffton, I had written papers and finished the final eight weeks of my other two elective classes at Bluffton, which were Interpersonal Communications and Coaching Methods. I finished them one at a time online. With the biology classes and labs, I could not simply write papers to complete the coursework. I had to be present. Since I was not driving on my own and going to rehab three days a week over an hour away from Bluffton, attending classes was simply not feasible.

After discussing this with my biology professors, we came to an agreement. Even if I got zeros on every test and assignment in those final weeks before graduation, I would still at least pass the classes because I had done well enough earlier in the semester. An enormous relief came after I realized I would be able to graduate with a Bachelor of Arts in Biology.

It was already two full years after I had been scheduled to graduate and I had just spent those years relearning how to take a simple step, so there was no way I wasn't going to walk to get my diploma. I planned to walk in the commencement ceremony on May 3rd, 2009.

During the ceremony, they announced to the packed football stadium to please hold all applause to the end. Upon hearing this, I was disappointed. Here I'd just had the fight of my life, and I was being told people cannot even clap for a few seconds on my behalf? Now, of course I recognized that everyone else at graduation was just as deserving, but it was a selfish moment for me. Secretly, I hoped nobody would listen to the holding applause request.

As I shielded my eyes from the glare of the bright midday sun on a cloudless warm day, I sat among the rows of graduates. After our row was dismissed to go up to the edge of the platform, my heart began to float but soon came back down. What about my teammates who were killed? They deserved to have this moment just as much as I did. Soon though, I had to focus on something else, taking the few steps over to the podium with the other graduates.

Once my name was finally called, I slowly climbed the stairs to the stage. The heavy weight I had been carrying around since the first day I attended classes at Bluffton University six years earlier was gone. Even after this metaphorical weight was lifted, my legs felt heavy. I was concerned I'd trip going up the stairs and ruin an otherwise perfect day. Not having navigated stairs too often in my rehab, my brain and body had to focus on the task at hand. I kept my head down, used my good right hand to hold on to the railing, and watched my feet slowly prod their way up the few stairs to the stage.

Next, I heard the resounding ovation and yelling. Since we were in a football stadium, it was as if I had just gone years preparing for a football game, made a big play, and the crowd was reacting.

A few of my college friends with whom I should have graduated were in attendance. One of those guys led the charge and immediately shot to his feet after my name was called and thus began an enormous ovation by the entire stadium.

This situation caused more mixed emotions. In a way, I was a bit nervous that authority figures at the graduation would calm everyone down because of the holding applause request. Another concern was for the rest of the graduates—I mean, they all had earned their moment, too. In my world though, the ovation was justified and deserved. It took two years of fighting like crazy to be able to even stand on my own. I had battled like a madman to be able to walk up a few simple steps. I scraped and clawed to receive a science diploma that science itself told me I was not supposed to finish.

Even though earning this diploma had taken a massive detour, it was now fully accomplished. When I reached the president of the university, he extended his hand. I took it, pulled him in, and gave him a hug.

Exiting the stage, I took my diploma and, seizing the moment, thrust it to the sky. This was my way of celebration, of thanking God for the miracle he had worked through me, but I was also telling my teammates who were killed, "This is for you."

As planned, I saw Doctor Relm again a little over a month after graduating Bluffton. Yes, the same guy who I thought must be a total quack. As I was waiting, I remembered I had seen this doctor before but couldn't remember exactly what for. I knew he was a brain doctor and I also recalled that, the last time I saw him, he did not prescribe any new medication or rehab. I thought I must have lucked out.

My heart fluttered as I sat there waiting, curious what new prescription or therapy he might *have* to prescribe this time. However, upon entering his light tone and warm smile made me forget my apprehension.

He had me reach out my finger and touch my nose. Not thinking about it, I did as he instructed without shaking. He then became overjoyed and quite animated. He pulled me in for a huge bear hug. I was confused as to why he was so excited— after all, I had only touched my nose. He reminded me about the first time I saw him.

Then it hit. I remembered the struggle it had been to hold my finger steady and touch my nose. I also remembered his prediction. The tremor was greatly improved. He was correct, and I had been wrong. This doctor was the furthest thing from a quack, and I had experienced yet another personal victory.

Bottom of the 8th
Personal Reflections

There is not a trace of quit in me, and yet, after hearing the neuro-psych results, I had begun to seriously doubt my potential to improve.

Emotionally speaking, I had taken a savage blow. I had subconsciously started to accept a bleak future. My thoughts included, *God, all my life I lived for being active. If this is all the improvement I can expect, why didn't you just take me instead of letting me live out my life like this?* I know lots of people with injuries may feel something like this, and I wish I could say something more of comfort or had an adequate answer to the question of how to resolve such dark feelings. All I can say is the Lord knows what's best and there is tremendous good that will eventually emerge.

From a purely scientific standpoint, there was no reason to continue fighting, or harbor any hope whatsoever. Science said I was no good. I had been a biology guy and I love science. Why would I doubt science and brain experts? I didn't know much about the brain, and those people with PhD's knew a lot more than I did. Logically, it made no sense to continue either.

I could have easily given up hope right then and there. When Trisha had protested the test findings, claiming they were "just not true," and Tonya had pounded on the table and forcefully hollered, "We are Bertas! We do not give up," I had become reenergized. Their spirited refusal to accept the limiting prognosis reminded me of the warrior I am. Once I heard them, the fierce fighter buried inside of me was resurrected.

At this point, I knew what I needed to do, but also knew how out of control my life seemed. I made the choice again to honor my deceased teammates. I remembered what my dad had told me. I was the only one who could put in the grunt work to change where I was. Once again, as I did in inpatient rehab, if the outpatient therapists told me to do five reps on an exercise machine, I'd do eight. If they told me to do eight reps, I'd do ten. This time, it wasn't to show "those people" that it was easy. These extra reps were done with the intention of improving quicker and maybe more than anyone had ever expected me to.

My entire family stepped up to the plate and did their best to help me recover. Our family meeting told me we were all in this together and we were going to fight for my future life, whatever that future life was. Yes, I had to do the grunt work to get out of this bus accident injury situation, but my family members were all going to support me, regardless of the outcome. All the members of my family were the most valuable players that day.

I made the choice to take control and *ownership* of my recovery and wanted to fight to get as much back as I could. By the grace of God, I was given a chance to improve my situation, and not all people who suffer brain injuries or accidents have that opportunity. My deceased teammates, along with my family, were with me, willing to fight alongside me and willing to support me if I was still fighting.

I was willing to fight alongside my immediate family, but my aunt and cousin helping me with speech was another story. I just don't have a good answer for not wanting the extra speech therapy at home and for being less than gracious for receiving it. I am ashamed to write about this, but I admit these occasions were not a highlight of my recovery days. I only thought about myself, and not my teammates, who didn't have a choice. I also did not consider the feelings of my cousin and aunt, who were both generously volunteering their time and energy to help me.

It was a dark time I am not proud of. I hope my aunt and cousin know how much I appreciate their willingness to work with me. I guarantee that, because of their help, I came much further along in recovering my speaking abilities. I would like to tell them both, along with my deceased teammates and their families, that this was a moment I let you all down, and for that I am deeply sorry. My aunt and cousin were right, and I was wrong. When I listen to my voice on video from that period, and recognize how terrible I sounded, I am especially humbled and regret not having been more welcoming of the gift and blessing I was being given.

Still, I must focus on the strides I made. I am only human.

Passing the second swallow test was a celebration for the ages and back to Red Lobster it was. Once again, it was just as good as before and I thoroughly enjoyed every morsel, down to the very last bite. This was especially true when it could be washed down with actual water, minus the thickener. Yes, I still had to tuck my chin and make sure I sat up straight. Both were strategies given by the occupational therapist, aunt, and cousin to make sure the water went to the right spot. To this day, I still consider this an epic meal and celebration.

This was also a time I needed all the boosting I could get. Having my original goals, plans, and dreams since early high school ripped out of my grasp at no fault of my own left me with no future, at least not one I had planned for or could envision as satisfying.

Around this time of relearning to walk independently in UTMC outpatient was when I realized the Lord was with me and hundreds, if not thousands, of people were praying for me. There were times I could literally feel the Lord was at my side. The only way to really know what I mean is to experience it, and I know some people have experienced this, too. It's not because I have more faith or am somehow more special than anyone. I had moments of weakness, and plenty of doubts and struggles, but people were praying, and at times, I could physically feel it.

Knowing that people were praying for me is what kept me going along with who I was at my core. When I found out how far it was to go a mile in the upstairs gym, I was all about it. In a time of accepting that none of my former goals were realistic, this small goal seemed worth going after. I now had a better understanding that my progress was all about baby steps, with the occasional breakthrough keeping me afloat. Once I had completed this modest goal, it paved the way for larger aspirations. Some of these large goals became speaking requests.

Around this time, the National Football Foundation and Hall of Fame Toledo chapter contacted me about winning The Don King Courage Award. This award was given to people who had overcome extreme obstacles and challenges in their life. I had won a scholar athlete award in football from that organization while in high school, so my earning this honor seemed like a perfect fit. What better recipient than a former scholar athlete award winner from that organization?

On the evening of the award, I gave an acceptance speech to the crowd of roughly three hundred people. The crowd included high school football inductees, their families, high school coaches, college coaches, and even a few of my outpatient therapists came.

To put it in football terms, my speech scored a touchdown to win the game. In baseball terms, I knocked that one out of the park. I talked about how my "teams," and I used courage to get me to the point I'm at today. I also spoke about working together—even the smallest, most seemingly insignificant member of a team can have a huge impact. I then invited all present to be a member of my team. There are only two positions on my hypothetical "team." To have courage and to be encouraging. Believe me, these aren't always easy. However, those are the only two positions on my team, and every single day is game day.

Afterward, there were many requests to speak in local churches, different organizations, community events, University of Toledo ceremonies and classes, Lourdes University classes, and numerous other events. I felt like I had achieved a victory in securing some purpose, and finally felt like my life was headed in a good direction.

———

There was a brain injury convention taking place in Columbus, Ohio. Since I was in rehab at UTMC, a woman who was a part of that organization had asked me if I would want to present something on the topic. I agreed and, after thinking about it, decided that I wanted to put together something that would help everybody in the audience relate to my circumstances. The idea came from an e-mail a friend had forwarded to me. I put together a presentation entitled "Seasons," which included the slideshow from that email.

The slideshow was the story of a man who sent each of his four sons to look at a tree. Each one looked at the tree during a different season and came back to report what they had seen. When they all reported different things, the man explained to his sons they were all correct in their observations, yet incorrect, because they had each seen only one season in the tree's life. Judging the tree by only one season does not give you the whole picture.

I related the different seasons of recovery following my brain injury to that story, describing such things as my Atlanta season in critical care, my wheelchair season, my inpatient rehab season, my outpatient rehab season, my dry drought season of being unable to drink thin liquids like water, and so forth. If you judged only one season of any brain injury recovery, you would get an incomplete picture. The audience of at least three hundred people was hanging on every word. I could tell, immediately after I finished, that they all wanted more. A rousing standing ovation began.

Suddenly, I could *see*. I could see speaking was an open door I had not considered before. I could see a future in doing this and hoped I would get the opportunity again. Speaking felt right. I felt calm. I felt relaxed. I felt at peace.

Now, even with a damaged brain and the loss of much athletic skill, lots of joy comes to me from speaking. At times, it feels like speaking is what I was meant to do. Yes, I am the same person who "forgot" he could speak. Yes, I am the same person that rebelled against my aunt and cousin for the extra speech work. Yes, I am the same person that thought I sounded just fine. I had no idea the importance my ability to speak clearly would play in my future. How ironic. But God knew and put the right people in my path. Praise the Lord that I can speak at all, with my brain injuries and the breathing tube being shoved down my throat after the accident. That life-saving action could have damaged my vocal cords irreversibly. The vocal cords are as fragile as butterfly wings and do not heal as readily as other body tissues.

The brain is another delicate piece of the human body, which is why it's heavily protected by the skull. The brain controls just about everything too, and it's almost scary how much power lies in the human brain. To understand the brain is to understand just about every body function. The brain is not completely understood by any human, and that's intimidating when you have an injured one. That's why I have a ton of respect for medical staff who work with brains, like Dr. Relm my neurologist.

Doctor Relm is amazing. From the first time I met him he was jovial, friendly, and optimistic about my future. In fact, one time I clearly remember sitting across a table from him and him pounding on that table, announcing, "With the injuries you sustained, there is no medical evidence telling me you should be where you are or doing what you're doing. This is a miracle."

It's especially powerful to hear him speak when he has his medical students come and examine me, and to watch their reactions. I go for check-ups about once a year.

In that moment of Doctor Relm telling me he was willing to bet that, given a year, the tremor would be gone without any rehab or medicine, I was baffled. Then, a year later, I had forgotten all about how he predicted my tremor would improve.

but I will never forget how I felt when he had me touch my nose again and his reaction. After Doctor Relm reminded me of my original visit for the tremor concerns, I was astonished. The brain had healed itself. The natural healing of the human body and brain is miraculous. By the same miracle working power of God, I was able to graduate Bluffton and move forward in life when science told me it was not possible.

9TH INNING

Top of the 9th
New Positions, New Fields
May 2009 - January 2015

Once rehab began to display massive advancements in everything toward the beginning of the second year following the bus accident, my parents and I began to talk about my future. A big issue was whether I would be able to drive, which was a big unknown. What the plan was after my rehabilitation ended was largely still a mystery.

Granted, nobody knew where it would end or how much further we had to go, but rehab was beginning to make a huge difference in improving my functionality. I was becoming more and more independent in dressing, showering, eating, and everyday life tasks. This meant a positive and fulfilling future was beginning to look like a real possibility. I had a plan, a goal, and a dream of what my life was going to be like before the accident. After the accident, I still desired those things, even if they seemed distant. I knew achieving those things meant a lot more school and work ahead of me, and of course that was intimidating. From life lessons though, I understood that if you want something, you must go after it and put in the work to achieve it.

Since I had now graduated from Bluffton, my parents and I began to discuss what was next. Mom and Dad would say, "Well, in case you forgot, the offer from Lourdes University still stands. You've already been accepted. Your aunt called us after receiving the acceptance letter when she was staying at our house while we were in Atlanta with you."

With a skeptical tone, I said, "I don't know, it's been a couple years since then."

"Yes, Tim, as far as we understand. I mean, we can call again, but as far as we know it still stands."

After it was determined the full scholarship at Lourdes University was still available, I made another choice. Granted, with already being accepted and the full ride option, the choice was an easy one. I didn't get hit in the head that hard. Still, deciding to go back to college, while not knowing how my brain would now function, was a formidable task, but it was the least I could do to honor my fallen teammates.

———

In January that year, the 44th President of the United States was inaugurated. That June, my sister, Tonya, graduated from Ida High School. She had been recruited by Siena Heights University to play softball and accepted the offer. The country was adjusting to new leadership, and Tonya and I were both headed for new schools and new futures.

That summer also marked the beginning of driving instruction for me at UTMC in an actual car. Before then, I had my vision and general knowledge tested, but now, much to my pleasure, it was time for a real vehicle. I awoke on the first day I knew I was going to start driving testing using an actual automobile and emotions of gladness and joyous anticipation began. Those feelings grew and grew as we arrived at the rehab center at UTMC. The delighted and eager feelings soon would become a wave of regret and anger.

The driving instructor asked for my driver's license. I had not needed it, or my wallet for years so hadn't even worried about grabbing it before leaving. He required that and would not take me out without it. After realizing the situation, my heart began to race, and my cheeks became as red as a sunburn. I was enraged.

Once again, my future was delayed, and things were taking longer than anticipated or desired. After I returned home that day and had to retell the disgusting story about not bringing my license, I got more and more angry until it wore me down. There was nothing I could do about it; the day had passed; the opportunity was missed, and I had no choice but to wait.

Another day, I remembered my license and we began driving instruction in the actual vehicle.

I would finally have the chance to prove myself. While walking out to the practice car, I remember thinking, *I wish that neuropsychologist could see this. Number one, I am walking on my own and, number two, walking to get into a vehicle to be tested for driving.* Those thoughts had me walking out to the practice car with a newfound swagger and no small amount of attitude.

Unfortunately, once I started relearning how to drive, I had difficulty multitasking. Watching the road and performing tasks such as turning on the windshield wipers or defroster while driving gave me a great deal of trouble. My left hand was far from working as it used to. Whenever I tried to quickly do something on the instrument panel, my focus would be lost, and the car would begin to drift. I also could not handle the car as well with only one good hand, which was especially obvious during parking maneuvers.

Toward the end of the summer, the occupational driving therapist was not seeing enough progress and needed a pause. His final plan and verdict? We would see where my still-healing brain and body were at when we resumed testing next summer.

Next summer? I sensed heat creep up from my toes to my forehead once again. I felt that thunderstruck sensation when for three times you have completely scoured over the list of those who made the basketball team only to realize your name is not there.

Once more, the future was not going to go the way or as fast as I assumed it would, and my dreams and hopes were dashed again. Here I thought I was going to be able to prove those neuropsychologists and their testing wrong and now I was being told to not practice at all and just wait around until next year.

As was usually the case throughout life, when things were not going my way, on the surface I kept cool. I shook the instructor's hand, saying, "Okay, I'll try to improve over the winter months."

In my head, I fumed, thinking what seemed to be obvious: *The only way I'm going to get better is if I drive! How can I get any better at driving if I don't keep driving?* I had been practicing driving with my parents when doing the back and forth from our house in Ida to rehab at UTMC, so I didn't see any reason to stop now. Wouldn't that just put me behind?

What are you thinking? My mind screamed at the occupational driving therapist, but neither he nor anyone else could hear my inner dialogue. Like before when things were not going my way, I kept my cool but had just been told to do what was usually not part of who I was—waiting for things to just get better or improve on their own was not how I operated in most situations. Almost my entire life had been spent attacking and fighting for what I wanted.

Regardless of my perceived failure in the driving class, I was determined to move forward and make progress in other, and perhaps more significant, areas of my life. So that fall I still began pre-nursing at Lourdes University.

After discussing the plan with my academic advisor at Lourdes, we decided that I would start by taking one class per semester. This made sense since there were no fees or tuition, and therefore, no deadline. I could take my time. Since I could not drive on my own, I would have to rely on whatever worked for my parents' schedule. We also had to devise a plan that included me still attending outpatient rehab. It only made sense to schedule one class in the evening, after my therapy, since Lourdes campus was on our way to and from the outpatient rehabilitation at UTMC.

The first course I registered for was a Research and Writing class that met one day a week for two and a half hours. I knew going to class immediately after rehab was not going to be easy on me, but I still fully intended and planned to move forward with my career as a nurse. I refused to let those high caliber, intense and challenging biology and chemistry courses at Bluffton go to waste.

To say it was frustrating figuring out how my "new brain" functioned is an understatement. Writing a research paper was my first major challenge. I did not yet fully grasp and was still not realizing the severity of my injured brain. Before my injuries, I could read a few pages and remember them. I would jot down some notes and remember the concepts. Now, because that method was all I knew how to do, I naturally resorted to the familiar.

As I tried to work on my research paper, it was soon obvious I could not perform as before. I did not know what to do or how best to operate without going back to previous experiences. I did know that my thoughts came incredibly and painfully slowly. I had to continually go back, read, reread, and dig to find information I had just read two or three minutes beforehand. Having to relearn how to learn was exasperating. It felt like I had started over in kindergarten. I had to learn how to learn again, and, this time, there were no apples.

These challenges made my brain injuries unmistakably real to me. They became concrete evidence of my brain issues as I was now trying to function in the "real world."

————

Outpatient rehab continued, and this massive rehab struggle was helping me to regain skills. I was still pursuing and showing improvements by persistently fighting every day even three years after the accident. Outpatient continued three days a week. That fall season slowly turned into winter and driving me to outpatient and Lourdes University became more difficult —we had to go slower and be more cautious with the snow and ice. While entering and exiting our house and the UTMC rehabilitation hospital or Lourdes, we had to be careful we didn't slip and fall. As soon as the snow seemed like it'd be there forever, its melting slush made cars on the roads filthy and wet.

Finally, the days started to become warmer and planting season had begun. I also continued to sow seeds of improvement in my own recovery at UTMC. I kept learning new things and regained a little bit more each day. Spring also marched on and after pools had begun to open and baseball season continued, I knew it was time for us to start driving instruction again. On the day I arrived at the hospital to begin driving training and made sure I had my driver's license, I told the therapist, "Well, I'm looking forward to it and I'll see what happens."

I was too fatigued from being angry and anxious all the time to assert myself beyond that. If driving was meant to be, it would be. If it wasn't meant for me, then I guess I would have to figure something else out. Just like drinking water, though, this by no means meant I didn't want it to happen—I wanted to relearn to operate a vehicle on the road so badly I could taste it. There was also my own voice in my head, saying, "I need be able to drive. I mean, what girl would want to date a guy who can't drive?"

The driving instruction process continued throughout that summer of 2010, with parking tests and all sorts of different driving tasks. My ability to safely use freeways, obey traffic laws, navigate parking lots, and even parallel park was tested just as it was before when I was first learning to drive as a sixteen-year-old. That season dragged on with what looked like favorable progress in my view, but time seemed to be running out.

In the last full month of summer that year, I received a call from my father. "Hey, Dad," I answered. "What's up?"

"Hi, partner. I just got off the phone with the driving instructor at UT."

"Yeah . . . And?" From the tone of his voice, my joyful expectancy grew. "What'd he say?"

Dad cleared his throat. "You've been released to drive. The therapist told me he has no hesitation in letting you get back on the road. You're completely safe and good to go."

I had no idea what to do. I wanted to go out right then and take a drive through the neighborhood, but I had no vehicle. I did know for sure that another mountain had been climbed and I had victory. I was regaining one more lost piece of my old life. The joy was unmatched, especially after having been told, with no uncertainty, that I would never drive.

One day, after Mom and Dad got home, I asked them about taking the van for a little joyride. Just as I'm sure they had been when I was a teenager, they were hesitant, but allowed me to go. I thought back to what my first solo trip was, from way back when I was sixteen or seventeen. I remembered that I had driven over to a friend's house. So, I decided to retrace the same route and drove Mom's van over to that same friend's house in Ida.

Driving was satisfying to say the least, and driving that same route was like a reset. It felt like things had come full circle, and I was back to starting out as a sixteen or seventeen-year-old.

———

Along with all these changes in my personal life, at Lourdes University, things began to change on campus. A decade after the Y2k scare, the institution began transitioning from Lourdes College to Lourdes University, while also introducing the first-ever intercollegiate sports teams.

In a remarkable coincidence, Bluffton University was called Bluffton College when I attended my freshman year and, during that year, began the change to Bluffton University as it is still known as today. It seems then, that if a college wants to become a university, the only thing they need to do is accept me into their school.

Once I knew Lourdes was adding sports, I felt as though I was back at Bluffton. Lourdes began with women's volleyball, men's basketball, and men's and women's golf and with time gradually added more. I'd be able to attend different university sporting events again and was especially looking forward to watching the baseball team. That is, of course, if the weather permitted. I don't do well at all in cold weather, while watching or playing.

———

Since a former inpatient physical therapist (scrubs lady) already had my contact information and was also an instructor at The University of Toledo, I was frequently asked to visit her physical therapy classes. Yes, she was one of the same inpatient physical therapists whom I had thought were trying to make me suffer. Of course, I had long since determined that it had been quite the opposite. She had me visit so that her physical therapy students could evaluate and assess me, and I was happy to oblige. When I visited her classroom, I made it a point to tell the students about the hatred I had for her, which certainly got more than a few laughs.

Time marched on.

Soon Hurricane Irene would hit the east coast of the United States. But far from the coast was The University of Toledo and "scrubs lady." Around this time, she and other doctors at UT decided to hold the first-ever White Coat Ceremony for students entering the Doctor of Physical Therapy School. They wanted a keynote speaker for the ceremony who had at one point been a physical therapy patient. They needed someone who could give a little bit of insight as to what physical therapy meant to them within the process of their recovery. I was selected and was delighted to tell the audience about my own personal hurricane. This meant I would have the honor of being the keynote speaker for the first Doctor of Physical Therapy White Coat Ceremony in the history of The University of Toledo.

In my speech, I mentioned how I hated physical therapy at first, which came because of not understanding its purpose. I spoke about feeling under attack by the therapists. I told the audience that, in the end, physical therapy had given me hope and helped me to reach my goals. I also mentioned how had it not been for the physical therapists' dedicated work, especially with the serial casting, I would not be walking today. After my catastrophic and life-altering permanent injuries, physical therapy really had impacted life for the better.

———

In the second year of having intercollegiate athletics, Lourdes had launched a baseball program along with a couple other sports at the start of that fall semester. One day, the first baseball coach in the history of Lourdes University asked to meet with me. We set out for the local ice cream shop, and he treated me to a "Monster shake." Talk about starting off on the right foot.

During our conversation, we talked about his baseball philosophies and strategies. That aspect is intriguing because the infield of each baseball field has the same dimensions and defensive positions, but strategies may be remarkably distinctive from coach to coach. The batting order and other offensive approaches may also be unique.

He told me that he believed in placing his best hitter third in the lineup. Some coaches use them at fourth, some put their best hitter in the second spot. I can see a benefit for each position in the line-up. A personal favorite philosophy of mine is that it's just better to have a great hitter at every spot in the line-up, so you don't have to worry about batting order. I'll let you know if I ever figure out how to do that . . .

Once our conversation began to wind down, I wished him good luck in the upcoming season. Finally, he said, "Well, Tim, you don't seem to be understanding, but I'm asking you to come on board and help me coach the team."

I stared at him in disbelief. It was quite an honor and flattering that he would ask me.

On the other hand, I was hesitant and wary of taking on such an obligation, thinking, *I don't know what that may entail, and my schoolwork is already going to be quite a lot on me.* From my experience with the writing class, combining sports with academics would be a much bigger challenge than it previously had in my life. I wasn't sure if splitting my time was a good idea anymore, with my brain injuries being what they were.

At the same time, I also found myself thinking, *Why do you want me? I can't do anything—I can't hit the infield warm-up, can't throw batting practice, and can't even play catch.*

He seemed genuinely interested in having me on board. I hesitantly agreed, but said, "I will give you what I can, which isn't much."

With that, I became one of the first two baseball coaches in the history of Lourdes University baseball. I did tell him right up front, however, "When you and the baseball team travel to away games, I'll willingly ride along. But if you travel on a bus to Florida for Spring Break, I will not go, and I'm sure you'll be just fine without me."

As the baseball practice that fall of 2011 progressed, I did what I could but, in all honesty, I could not do much. It felt as though I was letting the team down. That said, an important discovery was made. I realized that it was still crucial, for my mental wellbeing, to be a member of a team again. For as long as I can remember, being a major contributor as a part of a sports team was life. During this season, it did not feel as though I contributed and felt more of a bother and nuisance to the head coach or players.

The fall practice came and went, and soon we left school for Christmas break. Once we returned and practice for the season began the first month of next year, we needed to have indoor practice in a rec center in town big enough for infield practice in real distance.

Every time the team would begin playing catch, I'd scurry to find a batting helmet or move as far out of the area as I could. Being inside usually meant it wasn't possible to get far enough away so would often conveniently have to use the bathroom when they'd start. Terrified of getting hit in the head by a stray baseball, I did not want to take any chances. Even professional baseball players have throws that get away from them at times. Baseballs are hard things, too—I'd been hit by many over the years of playing and had a tooth or two need repairing after being split in half. With the new severe head injuries, dental concerns were the least of my worries.

On top of my fear of getting hit by the ball was the fact that I was not physically capable of hitting grounders or fly balls. I was also not physically capable of playing catch or throwing batting practice. I felt defeated and worthless. Plus, I was struggling with the morning practices seven days a week. Half the time was spent thinking about how tired I was and what I could not do. I went back to my old way of thinking about what I wished I could do but couldn't, instead of focusing on the good things, and finding joy in being a member of a college baseball team again.

As the practice and school year progressed, the day I had been dreading arrived. From the first time the head coach approached me about coaching baseball, I knew this day would come. Though I did my best to remain somewhat excited, I couldn't help experiencing it with a sense of gloom and a feeling of trepidation.

The Lourdes University baseball team was loading their bus to embark on their journey down to Florida for spring training. Even though I was not traveling on the bus, just as I had told the head coach right off the bat that I wouldn't be, I was filled with a deep, consuming anxiety. I boarded the bus to wish all the players a good and safe trip.

I felt torn in all directions. Though I did not remember anything from my ill-fated experience, I knew this was the same situation Bluffton had started out in. I kept telling myself, *Now, what are the odds of an accident like that happening again? I mean, the accident was a fluke thing, so why don't you just ride with them?*

As I stood on the stairs of the bus, amidst all the hustle and bustle of loading, it occurred to me how the players and other coaches might be viewing me. Here I was supposed to be one of their leaders but was too much of a coward to ride the bus down to Florida with them. I do not know what thoughts they may have had on the subject, but I filled in those thoughts for them—I figured at least some must have been along the lines of, *why would I listen to anything this chicken has to say? He's not even man enough to ride the bus with us.*

As soon as that dark projection crossed my mind, I told myself, *well, that's going to be how it is, and I'm sorry, guys. I hope you never have to deal with the feelings I'm dealing with right now, but I can't bring myself to ride the bus on the same trip again. Emotionally, it would simply be too much.*

So much for being part of the team—even five years later, and even though I recalled nothing, the emotions surrounding that event were still too raw. There were way too many similarities seeing college baseball players board a bus for a trip down to Florida, especially knowing what I had recently experienced and had a complete understanding of what could happen. Standing in the stairwell of the bus, I saw all the familiar emotions of the players embarking on the adventure together—excitement, anticipation, and pure happiness.

I scanned the inside of the bus and tried to remember where I had been sitting on the day Bluffton University had left. Just as quickly as the thought came, I wiped it out of my mind. It was just too much, so what was the point in going there? Before exiting the bus, I turned around and announced, "I love you, guys." To which a resounding response of "We love you too, Coach!" came back from the team.

A month or two before this, the athletic director and I had talked. She and her husband were flying down to Florida at the same time, and she let me know that I'd be welcome to join them on the flight. If I did that, I could join the team, and that's what I did.

As I watched the bus pull away, I knew it was time to get ready for my trip.

Unexpectedly, packing for the flight had been a big mental drain. Not having been on airplanes a whole lot in general, and certainly not since my accident—other than the time I was out of it when being transferred from Atlanta to Toledo—I was uncertain about what I would need to keep in my carry-on and what I could pack in my suitcase and send along on the bus. While packing and trying to keep things in my head, at one point I just had to sit down.

My brain was unexpectedly overloaded. Writing items down on a list and crossing them off was not really a viable option either. Since I was by myself, it was a chore just to write simple words, and I could not always read my chicken scratch. I did print off a sheet with items, but then shortly lost the sheet. Little did I know, these symptoms of not thinking too clearly, and unsteady hands, were more than likely the beginning of something I had not yet experienced. Something exceedingly unhealthy.

After touching down and exiting the plane in sunny Florida, I breathed in the sunshine.

At some point, I remember thinking about my teammates from Bluffton University who were killed. "Well, I made it," I told them. "It took me a long time." I took in another deep gulp of Florida air. "I made it, guys. The weather is just fine, and I wish you were here."

I looked back north in the direction of Atlanta and paused, feeling joyful relief filled with curiosity, but also much sorrow.

———

After being in pre-nursing at Lourdes for a few years, it became obvious that nursing would not be a wise move for my future. Even with campus resources and tutors at my disposal, and the fact that I was only taking one class per semester, I was not managing the type of work required. I mentally did not have the stamina for lengthy classes and certainly not for the long shifts as a nurse even if I could somehow graduate.

I could not always perform certain tasks even with both hands, and simply could not function as quickly or accurately as would be required, especially when any emergency situations arose. Those traits would be imperative for nursing. Standing for long periods of time didn't suit me well either—my left leg would simply become sore and stiff quicker than it used to. It was incredibly frustrating to need to sit down more frequently.

To add to those difficulties, my hands were limited at best. My left hand was not as flexible or strong or easily controlled. My left fingers were stiff. Even my good right hand, while greatly improved, would begin to shake at rare times while performing simple tasks. This shaking was particularly apparent when I was fatigued, which was often. Also, without a spleen, it did not seem like a good idea to be around sick people all day. The spleen is part of the body's immune system.

Regardless of how hard I tried to concentrate; my mental capacity was not what it had been. After only three classes in the pre-nursing curriculum, the fact my new brain or body was not up to the high-level requirements was apparent.

I could no longer become a nurse. I did not know how to handle this and felt beaten and useless. Giving up the dream I had ever since I began to consider careers was one of the most difficult choices I've ever had to make. It felt like a defeat and appeared as though the neuropsychologist's test had won out in the end.

Since becoming a nurse was the only job I had ever considered, I had no other ideas. All my schooling, training, thoughts, time, and money were spent with the eventual goal of becoming a nurse anesthetist. Now that dream was gone, and I felt lost.

Those feelings hung around like heavy rain that will not let you out of sight. The sentiments remained until something unexpected came along, providing an answer. Perhaps I seemed more lost than usual walking around campus, and someone noticed, or perhaps it was just fortuitous timing—I don't know —but a few faculty members suggested that, since I had finished my undergraduate degree at Bluffton, I apply to the graduate school at Lourdes University.

I thought, *Graduate school? I don't know if I can do that.* I mean, the undergraduate courses I took at Bluffton were difficult enough, even with a healthy brain. Classes at Lourdes, especially at the graduate school level, would certainly be challenging with this new brain.

When wrestling with this, I also considered something else. If I didn't go after graduate school and at least give it "the old college try," I would always wonder if I could have done it and regret not trying. Science said I was defeated before I even began. What did I have to lose? My deceased teammates deserved this. Lourdes was willing to help me, and I made a choice.

I chose a Master of Organizational Leadership degree. The fact it would be graduate-level schoolwork was intimidating. The fact I was told by the neuropsychologists going after any new degree would end in failure was daunting. In fact, according to the neuropsychologist's test, I had already failed, graduate degree or not. Sure, the fear of failing yet again could be felt, but I was still willing to try. Perhaps this was because I was attempting to go after something for more than just me, something that felt bigger than myself.

I talked it over with my parents, explaining my reasoning for not continuing to go for nursing. Describing the facts of being immune compromised, and my brain or body not being up to the task.

Knowing the dream had been in my heart for a long time, it was disheartening for my parents to see their son give up his long-term goal, the one they knew I had my heart set on. Mom was not convinced I'd made the right choice. She asked me what I was going to do with a Master of Organizational Leadership degree.

I then pulled out a sheet provided by Lourdes giving a long list of possible options, and the many varied directions it could possibly take me in. It could lead me into different aspects of the business field, education field, healthcare field, general management, and speaking, just to name a few. I had already given it a lot of thought and was going to go after it. My parents could see my heart was set, so they wanted to support me.

After our first collegiate baseball season at Lourdes University that spring, graduate school classes began that autumn. During my graduate school classes, and even during important tests, group work, and projects, my mind would wander. Although not constant, I would sometimes be thinking about where I would have been had these injuries not happened. It was easy to speculate, given the timeline and knowing, had it not been for the day that sealed my fate, I would have graduated Bluffton in 2007.

Irrelevant questions swirled in my head. *Assuming the accident had not happened where would I be now? I would have passed my undergraduate nursing classes, but I wonder where I would be living or working. Would I be in school for graduate-level nursing? Would more schooling not have worked out with my finances or schedule? I'm guessing I would have been done with schooling by now... So, would I be working my dream job, married and with a child or two? I bet my wife would be gorgeous.*

Either way, there was no reason to assume I would not be attending the graduate level nursing school, or maybe even finished by now. What or where I could have been ate at me. But I also knew that sometimes you must let things go to benefit the future, just like giving up playing baseball at Bluffton. As difficult as letting go may be, from time to time, you need to make that choice. It was a mental battle to do just that and focus on the reality—and the questions and answers that *were* relevant.

While in graduate school for leadership, my course load was not lightened—which was just the way I expected to be treated. Per UT medical recommendations, the school provided me with note takers during class along with extra time on tests. I continued passing each paper and class as I progressed through my graduate school program. The sweet smell of victory began ever so slightly wafting in.

There were times when struggling with demanding course work while coaching baseball had me wanting to give up. Often, there was a piece of me saying, *Why don't you just quit? What are you doing? Who do you even think you are? There's no point in trying to go any further, science says you're not going to accomplish anything else the rest of your life. You've studied science and you're a smart guy, so why are you resisting what appears to be the infallible truth?*

Still, another piece of me said, *Maybe I can't become a nurse, as I had always dreamed of, but I am alive, so I am meant to do something—something more than sitting around and feeling sorry for myself.*

Graduate school would give me lots of opportunities not previously considered. Even though it was not nursing school, it was graduate-level coursework, and that made me feel like me again. I came to terms with the fact that my injuries might not allow me to go as far as I had wanted to on the path "old Tim" had once been on, but I was still going to go as far as possible on my new path. I made up my mind. "New Tim" was going to succeed in whatever capacity he could.

I knew according to the neuropsychologist's evaluation that going after this graduate degree would end in failure. I embraced this, having been an athlete and competitor my whole life. Every time you begin a game, there is a chance you will fail or get beat.

This makes it all the sweeter if you do come out on top. With my eyes set on the end goal, the hours of reading and looking over notes and pouring over papers were somehow comforting. The whole process of continuing my schooling and moving forward made me feel as though the accident and rehab and challenges were only unavoidable massive detours. Somehow, I was back to who I once was.

At Lourdes, I put in place a strategy used throughout life.

Win everything.

If I get up on time, I win. If I make my bed and brush my teeth, I win. If I make it to practice on time, I win. If I help with drills, I win. Once I make it to lunch, I win. If I see a tutor to help with my schoolwork, I win. If I work on the next paper's title page or works cited and get them correctly formatted, I win.

With each new paragraph I accomplished writing in each paper that I wrote, I'd try to win. Such was my life, trying to win at every aspect, even when it came to the small things—things most people don't even think about. I knew a lot of what I had been through and what I needed to do to function but knew nothing of the new health storm creeping in on my horizon.

I was speaking, helping coach baseball, working in residence life as a hall director with rotations on duty, and attending grad school. All of that certainly makes for a full plate.

It might have been too much. After about a year into graduate school and while still assisting coaching college baseball, two things took place. The first, I began to date a young woman. The second was, for reasons unknown, my thyroid gland went berserk.

The thyroid gland is a tiny gland located near the throat that aides with digestion. The worst part about my thyroid disease was that it didn't occur in a sudden burst, where it would have been noticeable, and I might have done something about it more quickly. Instead, it got worse and worse, at an extraordinarily slow pace. I did not know anything was even wrong for about half a year.

At the six-year anniversary of the accident, I had begun to exhibit troubling signs of a disease. Hyperthyroidism causes the food ingested to run through the body. This results in rapid weight loss. Food is not inside the body long enough to contribute any nutrients or anything beneficial in general.

As far as what caused my hyperthyroid, it could have been the brain healing from my previous severe injuries. The brain controls the thyroid. It could have been the stress of heavy graduate school classes while I was an assistant baseball coach and working occasional duties as an on-campus Resident Director or speaker at different classes or events. It could have been lack of sleep or rest in general, especially with the early morning baseball practices seven days a week. Jumping at the chance to be a part of a team again, I didn't take any days off to adequately recover.

At that time, I had a lot of stressors in my life. The start of the thyroid problem also could have been something completely different from anything I just suggested or a combination of all the above—I won't ever know for sure.

As that year progressed and the thyroid slowly got worse, I still had no idea anything was wrong. All I knew was that I was becoming enormously irritated at people telling me to go to see a doctor because of the weight loss. That annoyance just cemented even more my unwillingness to see a doctor. I was slowly becoming thinner, even though I was eating much more than usual. I constantly had no energy, and was weak, touchy, and acting extremely immature.

I kept telling myself, I just needed to eat more, and I would be fine. Besides, I was in grad school, for the first time in years I was dating a new young woman and was part of a college baseball team again—I was just starting to get my life back and had no time to mess around with seeing a new doctor. It was denial.

Yes, I was losing weight, but I was also not being me. Whenever anyone made a good-natured joke toward me or something else regarding me like, for instance, sports teams I rooted for, or when anyone poked fun at me in other harmless ways, it felt like a personal attack.

I remember another instance when I was sitting on the bed and staring at nothing, too wiped out to do anything or even think about anything. It's difficult to imagine being too tired to think, but that's how I felt in early 2013.

January through the end of April was college baseball season, so I was supposed to be enjoying it, yet, each morning, the first thought that came to me was, *I can't wait to get back to bed.* Any sleep I did get did nothing to rejuvenate me. The exhaustion and mental strain felt like defeat every single day. With the rapid and uncontrollable weight loss, it was as though my body was eating itself from the inside.

That college baseball season ended as soon as nice warm weather began to be a regular occurrence in northwest Ohio. As summer rolled on with my health deteriorating, the young woman I had begun to date left me. With my unmanageable digestion issues, I soon began to wet the bed every night.

Many days, my heart was racing as though I had just completed a mile run when I had not even exercised. I had no clue what was wrong and felt abandoned, alone, and once again it seemed my life was falling apart. I became gravely concerned, angrily thinking, *Great, I survive being thrown off a bridge, the lung surgery, and all the rehab, and, as soon as I'm starting to get back to life the way I want it, something else goes wrong. What gives?*

At the low point of this mystery illness, I had lost about fifty-one pounds, rapidly falling from a healthy 170 pounds on a six-foot-one-inch frame down to 119 pounds. I was not getting adequate sleep due to wetting the bed or getting sufficient nutrition because of having a bowel movement after every single meal. I was saying and acting out in immature, hurtful, and inappropriate ways. My heart was constantly beating out of my chest, and I would get so desperately angry about silly, inconsequential things that my hands would start shaking.

After my health got bad enough and I finally decided to get checked out and went to the urgent care, the doctors diagnosed thyroid problems. As it turns out, my thyroid was in such a terrible condition, when I finally got in to see the thyroid doctor, he labeled it a "thyroid crisis." Medications were prescribed to reverse the symptoms I was struggling with.

After the heavy dose of medications started to work by trick-or treating time that year, my health began to slightly improve. Besides the full ride and all the support, there were other good things at Lourdes University which kept me going.

———

An undergraduate student and softball player at Lourdes was a part of the on-campus Red Cross. From attending a conference over the summer, she got the idea of an "in honor of" blood drive. Her idea became the Red Cross blood drive in honor of Tim Berta. It was to be the first annual blood drive in honor of me and would take place during the fall semester of 2014.

My long-ago plans of being a nurse had me assuming I would be helping injury or illness victims in a completely different way, but I was saving lives even without being a nurse. I knew that if people had not given blood in Atlanta, I would not be alive. To know these donors were going to help future patients in my situation was overpowering and at times I needed to sit down. Emotions welled up inside of me as I looked around at all the people in line to give blood. What made it all the better was I knew they were giving blood in honor of me, in honor of the positive impact I'd had on others —in honor of the encouragement I'd given, the smiles I had shared and the inspiration I've become to everyone struggling through life in some way. All of this was made possible only because others gave blood, which saved my life. That's sobering.

I didn't give blood myself that day. I was dealing with my thyroid issue, and I was on heavy thyroid medications. I would get exceptionally worn out very easily. I reasoned then that giving blood was not a good idea, especially for driving purposes.

Talking and chatting with the people who were giving blood, however, filled me with great joy. Feeling the love and support from the entire Lourdes community felt like the acceptance I had desired my whole post-accident life. The goal was to collect thirty-nine units, and at the end of the day we had collected fifty-four. This was more than a single game victory —this was a winning streak beyond any I've had before.

My final year of graduate school at Lourdes gave me other great opportunities. I spoke to freshman introductory classes as well as nursing classes, and then there were other noteworthy times as well. In January 2015, before baseball season began in a couple weeks, I sat on the sidelines with the Lourdes University Men's basketball team during a game. I was an honorary coach.

Before we took the team out on the court, the head coach introduced me to the team by saying how touched and impacted he was by our very first meeting. He told the team that he had read books and listened to speakers, but that he had never learned as much from any of them as he did from just interacting with me. He also told them you cannot control what happens to you, but the important thing is how you respond to it.

As he was saying these things, it felt like a piece of the acceptance of an athletic team I craved ever since the accident.

Bottom of the 9th
Personal Reflections

Once it was determined how I'd get to Lourdes and the time of day I would need to schedule class, it was game time. The beautiful thing was I didn't have to worry about anything else. I did not have to worry about getting myself to rehab, or to Lourdes—Mom was going to drive me there on Thursdays after rehab. Mom gave of herself for my benefit. Mom was MVP for her years of taking off work and giving up income to drive to rehab most of the time.

I also didn't have to worry about paying for college, because Lourdes University had generously offered the very first full ride in the history of the school. Now, did I have to pay? You betcha, but not in the form of money to Lourdes—I had to pay it in about three and a half to four years of life being completely controlled by my injury and rehabilitation. I had to pay for it with permanent life altering injuries that will forever modify my life in other ways, even though my official rehab had ended. I had to pay for it in how my life goals and timeline were forever altered. I had to pay for it knowing teammates had been killed. I had to pay for it knowing that my scars—mental, emotional, and physical—would never fully heal.

Some days, I felt like I'd bitten off more than I could chew, much like learning to eat again had me doing. Talk about a challenge—physical, occupational, and speech rehabilitation along with college classes certainly made for a full day.

However, attending a college class, no matter how tired I was after a long day of rehab, made it feel like I was doing something for others with life, just like before with going to school so that I could save numerous lives. The only difference was now I knew exactly who I was working for. This was for all my teammates, for their families, and for everybody affected by the Bluffton University baseball team bus accident. The way I thought of it, any improvement that came was also for them.

The baseball field at Bluffton is now called Memorial Field. It has a sculpture outside the right field fence that honors the deceased players called "Circle of Remembrance." In the center of the circular sculpture is a home plate with the cleat prints of the five players killed imprinted on all five sides of that home plate.

Then, around that plate, there are the handprints of the survivors. It is a beautiful sculpture that causes me to feel mixed emotions. One emotion—and one that I will always experience—is sadness their lives were cut short. They still had their own dreams and whole lives ahead of them. At the same time, I am grateful that I have made such tremendous progress in my recovery. Progress science told me was impossible. God had other ideas. That thankfulness for my comeback gives me a sense of victory for my fallen teammates.

One of those improvements was driving, and what science said was impossible—God gave me the ability to fight tooth and nail for to earn back. Upon learning I could drive on my own, I felt like I had been released from prison. These days, when driving, always in the back of my head are the blunt words from that PhD. Her cold, uncaring words make driving and the freedom of the open road all the sweeter. That is only one example of many that make me thankful for what God has done for me and grateful for my perseverance in the face of what seemed impossible.

Yes, I relearned to drive, but I didn't feel good enough to be a college baseball coach. I felt unwanted and fearful, especially because I had to wear my batting helmet for the whole practice. I couldn't play, so I felt useless. No longer being a healthy and capable athlete had left a large hole coaching could not fill. I was exposed to something I had loved, and now could never fully partake in again.

It was another paradox. I was feeling empty that I couldn't play and insignificant as a coach but was counting my blessings in terms of still belonging to part of a college team. Being a part of a college baseball team again aided mental and emotional healing.

The Lourdes University baseball team leaving on the bus for the trip to Florida was a further contradiction of feelings for me. I was happy for the team, and excited for all the things they were excited for. A different piece of me was scared. I knew they were about to embark on the same ride I had taken just five years before. A journey that forever changed my life.

From the neuropsychological evaluation, I knew keeping in shape was crucial. Even though I was no longer a college athlete, I was a part of Lourdes campus. I could exercise on my own in their cardio and weight room. I did the same treadmill and elliptical workouts from outpatient. I still wanted to stay physically fit. For every aspect of my health, staying physically fit was vital.

One part of "old Tim" was fitness, but another part was academics and an emphasis on achieving in scholarly pursuits. That part of me was bummed because what I had been studying, sacrificing, and preparing for over the course of many years was no longer an option. It appeared those high caliber biology, math, and science classes were all for nothing.

Even though I had those thoughts in mind, I still tried to

focus on the fact God had worked a miracle in my life. I was happy I could do what I could. Yes, my original plans were shattered after the accident, but I could exercise, attempt to golf, drive, see, hear, read, learn new things, walk, dance (not too well, but that's beside the point), drink water, and eat solid food. And date! Not too bad for somebody who was thrown off a bridge at freeway speed.

What made it even more enjoyable is knowing the neuropsychologist's predictions based on the test were wrong. That proves doctors, although they are experts in their respective fields, can give a patient a prognosis, but cannot look into a person's soul and see their will to live. They certainly cannot stop God from performing miracles.

When I speak and encourage others, it provides me with an indescribably positive feeling. Speaking to the nursing or therapy classes or sharing my testimony in different churches came to feel as though it was what I was meant to do. It may be a long way from what was originally planned, but it is no less valuable. I intended on saving lives in another way but have touched hundreds through my speaking and hope to grow that number in the future. ESPN allowed me to touch even more lives by featuring a segment on the *E:60* show. These days, that feature is online on vimeo.com called *Remember Bluffton*. There is a link in the notes.

Being a former college athlete, I'm pleased I have had a chance to be on ESPN. I am glad, even though I would rather it have been for something else, like winning the Heisman trophy or making a big play in the World Series, and not the tremendous challenges and injuries sustained from an auto wreck.

However, what matters at the end of the day is I am trying to honor fallen teammates, a much bigger and more important undertaking than any I had ever imagined for myself.

The blood drive held in my honor, speaking to classes, and guest coaching, made time at Lourdes University much sweeter. Yes, my official time as a student at Lourdes has ended, but I love to stay involved and be on campus as often as possible. Today, I sit on the Alumni Board of Lourdes, and work with student athletes. I speak to classes, and volunteer there often. I make it a point to give back to the university that gave so much to me.

While in graduate school at Lourdes, I was usually bubbly, talkative, and friendly. Once my hyperthyroid crisis hit, all that changed. In fact, friends have since said, "It was like your light went out."

As I like to say, there is no tiredness like thyroid-tired. The thyroid-tired takes everything out of you and leaves you with complete emptiness, even joy is ripped out of your grasp. My heart aches for those I hurt during my thyroid crisis—you know who you are. I said things that were hurtful and did things out of character for me. At times, I became a monster.

Please understand, I did not know it, but I was very sick. I should have listened and gone to a doctor. I ask from the bottom of my heart for forgiveness. Talk about a letdown. Right when I had started to get back to life the way it was, something else hit me full force and knocked me down. This was another stretch of time where I got miserable and distraught. I remember being angry at God again. *Oh, so apparently the brain injury didn't get the message across, and now I must deal with this. What kind of "good plan" is this? What did I do wrong?* Once more, it felt like my best was just not good enough.

I was mistaken again. God is not in the business of retribution or punishment; God is in the business of restoring. God certainly took care of me after the world beat me up more than once. My thyroid and weight are much healthier now with the medication. That situation has improved beyond what the doctor originally predicted and told me. Sound familiar? God does not owe me any explanation for issues in life. I understand that, when problems come, God has my back, despite the difficult moments that once convinced me otherwise.

Getting a chance to attend graduate school was the culmination of my life's hard work. My efforts and sacrifices ended up being worth it, and not a waste of time after all. God was at work again in my life, and I am forever grateful. Even though I had no control over the bus accident, and it may not seem "fair," I looked at what I did have control over, what I still possessed and made a choice. I took personal responsibility to recover as much as possible and go after a better future and life for myself and for others. Just as "old Tim" had been doing.

I am not defined by what happened to me or any achievement, accomplishments like records eventually go away. I am who God says I am. One game may be over, but there's still a lot of ball left to be played. God gave me a chance to hit a walk-off grand slam in the bottom of the ninth to win the World Series. And winning the World Series is not as big as writing this book—a book written to honor my teammates lost.

This is for you, Zachary Arend, David Betts, Scott Harmon, Cody Holp, and Tyler Williams. May you each rest in peace.

EXTRA INNINGS

May 16th, 2015
Walk Off Grand Slam

We had picked up my cap and gown a few days beforehand. I tried it on once or twice just to look at myself in the mirror while wearing it. As I looked at myself wearing the master's degree graduation outfit, I began to ponder. Just as when I had graduated from Bluffton, teammates who were lost came to mind. What about them? What right do I have to be standing here? Science says I should be dead.

I wiped those thoughts away as quickly as they came. I'm meant to be here, and I'm honoring them. I'm honoring God, who helped me through. I'm honoring my family and friends who aided me all the way. I'm honoring myself—the me that fought like a rampaging bull to get to this point. Every step of the way presented an opportunity to honor my lost teammates, and I have done my best to do that.

Upon arriving at the Convention Center in downtown Toledo, Ohio, the enormity of the situation hit. As I waited in the side room where the rest of the graduates were, I took pictures with and chatted with other graduates. Many warm hugs were exchanged.

I had started graduate schoolwork not long after being told I'd never learn anything new or even be able to walk, but now I was going to graduate and walk across the stage after earning a master's degree. It was a little surreal. Science is only as good as the humans who research and record it. This science was completely wrong, and God had other plans for me.

Many friends and family came, since there was no limit to the number of guests a graduate could invite. I did not know it at that moment but, after the ceremony, I learned that lots of extended family had come to the graduation, some even from as far away as the Upper Peninsula of Michigan. I also did not know that some of my friends from Bluffton would be making the trip and was surprised and pleased to find them there as well. I met great people at Bluffton.

After us graduates had entered the main room of the enormous convention center just before the graduation ceremony, my sister, Tonya, was walking by with my 93-year-old grandma. As we passed them, Tonya stopped and gave me a hug and kiss on the cheek. That was an tremendously reassuring family moment that I will never forget. It was also encouraging that there was no request to hold any applause for any graduate.

Soon my cohort's turn came to line up at the bottom of the stage. Just as at Bluffton, as we climbed up the stairs, I was very focused on looking at the steps to keep balance. These stairs were steeper and higher than the stairs at the Bluffton ceremony. In my world, this felt very appropriate—in a symbolic sense—since this was a graduate degree and not a bachelor's. Upon reaching the top, I looked out in the crowd. Due to the glare of the bright lights, and the dark space beyond, it was impossible to see. Before long, I realized my turn was coming up next.

They called the graduate in front of me and thus began a wave of emotions in anticipation. Happiness, relief, joy, elation, disbelief, and satisfaction all rolled into one. After my name was called, I did a little dance, not much of one, but it felt like walking on air.

Before I stepped in front of my graduate school professor for the hooding, I thrust my fist down toward the stage with such force my cousin who was present later said he thought I was going to fling myself off the stage. Had I thrown myself off the stage, I think I would've been able to float. I felt that light. Everyone in the Convention Center had stood up as I was standing there getting my hood, and I started shaking my head in disbelief and pure joy.

I've never been much of a crier, but I couldn't help but let a few tears well up.

Now the bright lights were not the only reason I couldn't see—there were also the small tears. They were tears for everything that had happened. Tears for teammates killed, who did not have this chance, and tears for their families. Tears for what my whole family had been through. Tears for all the pain, struggle, miracles, loss, desperation, hopelessness, and all-encompassing fight. There were tears of personal joyfulness and ecstasy and tears for proving people wrong.

This was a moment for the ages. I had driven myself to my own graduation ceremony when science said I would never drive. I had walked across the stage when science said I would never walk. I had accepted a graduate diploma when science said I would never again learn new things.

I've recovered better than any science textbook would have dared to predict because of the Lord's strength, and not just my own. Yes, I kept up the fight and continued plowing ahead, but knowing the nature of brain injuries and that sometimes traumatic brain injuries (especially severe ones) will simply stop improving, I know it was not all me. My brain continued healing beyond what is "typical." I am an ordinary person, but my brain repaired itself in an extraordinary way.

The perfect people were in position at the perfect time and in the perfect place. Beginning all those years ago with Bluffton scouts at Ida High School, then me stopping in coach Grandey's office about quitting baseball, then the timing and location of the accident only to name a few. I could never have planned all of that and made them work together. With God's help, this trauma has offered me plenty of personal victories I would not have experienced otherwise.

I do not allow myself to dwell within the victim mentality. Yes, there were, and are, times I feel sorry for myself. Like my dad said, "You have every right to feel cheated and be angry, but only you can fix this."

However difficult or small it may be, I make the choice not to complain about what happened or the unfairness to all involved. Instead, I strive to find joy every day, even when joy feels distant. With help from the Lord, I have done my best to use this tragedy to bless people and make the best of what I still have to offer, which is a lot.

I have tremendous compassion for others and deep empathy for head trauma. I visit brain-injured patients as often as possible when I'm asked. I also have a vast amount of gratitude for the small things I am capable of, like using the toilet or showering on my own. Being able to eat typical food or drink thin liquids such as water with no issues or taking a simple walk all fill me with an immense thankfulness, much more than before. I have also come to a deeper level of faith and trust in the Lord. Despite my numerous failures and flaws, I know the Lord was there during my recovery and is with me every day. This gives me peace and joy beyond anything I've ever experienced.

Throughout this entire traumatic life event, no matter how low my confidence could be or how sick or sore I was at different moments, ultimately, I had faith in meeting my goals. I did not stay focused on where I was or how I felt, I looked at what I wanted and where I wanted to go. Sometimes you have to play through pain if you want to be successful.

A lot of this faith comes from my childhood experiences—like the pop jug. A lot of this faith comes from knowing I have the love and support of many family members and true friends. A lot of this faith comes from knowing with absolute certainty the Lord is with me. Yes, I still have plenty of challenges ahead, and many trials will knock me down.

Since some of my teammates can no longer make choices on this earth, I make a choice every day to honor them. This hole I have climbed and crawled out of, sometimes holding on by my fingernails, was all to honor my teammates killed, and I hope I did good, guys. This is for you. I have run the bases, crossed home plate and with the help of the Lord through many prayers, I have won. God helped me in turning what I thought was my greatest defeat into a decisive victory.

Martin Luther King Jr. once said, "The ultimate measure of a man is not where he stands in moments of convenience and comfort, but where he stands at times of challenge and controversy."

I have been defeated, time and time again, but will keep striving for greatness in whatever may come my way. Regardless of my many doubts and shortcomings, God has tremendously blessed me through this. I do not know what the rest of my life will hold, but I do know if I continue to be who I am and the man God made me to be, then I will honor my fallen teammates. That way, whether I win or lose the small battles, with the Lord, I will and already have victory.

POST-GAME FIREWORKS

Without the help of plenty of people, this memoir would not have been possible.

Thank you to my family for fighting alongside me. Thank you for sticking with me the whole way through my brain injury recovery. I know you love me and will always be there. I had lots of extended family help in Atlanta and at home. A mere "thank you" does not even begin to express the tip of the iceberg in terms of my feelings of gratitude. Both of my cousins helped in Atlanta early on, Aunt Jane, Uncle Corey, Aunt Lucy, Cousin Ruth, great Uncle Troy and Aunt Kay, and those are just a few. Mom, Dad, Trisha, and Tonya all had their own individual, unique massive impacts on my recovery as well.

Mom, you challenged and raised me in a way that prepared me for life. You gave up a lot of income by taking time off work to drive me to rehab. You also prepared a literal mountain of meals throughout the years, both pureed and in their typical solid form. That's an incredible sacrifice. Thank you.

Dad, you were just as important, and knew God was speaking to you through the bush in our backyard. It also must have been incredible observing my brain move. Thank you for fighting for me; you will always be my partner.

Trisha, I don't know how you were able to juggle everything going on with me while at the same time attending nursing school, but you knew just what to do to motivate me to move my arm. You won; I cheated. Thank you for all your support over the years and thank you for helping me.

Tonya, I feel awful for you having your high school years interrupted by my accident and recovery, and I'm sorry for that. By holding that bucket under my mouth, you made the clean-up process in the van much easier. This was especially meaningful to me because it was my first day of outpatient rehab. I want to deeply thank you for everything else along the way you contributed. I am glad you are still by my side; you make my life better. Thank you for encouraging me, and for believing I was worth it.

To my aunt and cousin, who worked with me on speech even when I didn't want to, thank you. My speech massively improved thanks to you both.

To Bluffton University, who gave me a great education, college athletic experiences, and friends for life; I am forever grateful. In 2017, our first year of eligibility, the 2007 baseball team was voted in and inducted to the Bluffton University Athletics Hall of Fame. It's a privilege to be recognized in such a manner. That too is "preserved behind glass for all to see." If somebody would have told me as a freshman, "Hey, a team you're a part of is going to be in the Bluffton University Athletics Hall of Fame," I'd have said, "Wow, then we're going to have to work really hard." I didn't think that the hard work would include basically relearning everything.

To my many friends who were there for me, especially the ones who came down to Atlanta to help. It is incredible Josh Green my Bluffton roommate was in Atlanta the very next day after the accident. Mike Smith and others from Bluffton along with friends from Ida came later as well. I have a tremendous amount of gratitude for all of you. My parents say what an incredible asset it was for all of you to be there. I'm told that, when you would play card games in my hospital room in Atlanta, even though I was completely out of it, you would deal me in. You also included me in your March Madness bracket. They along with family began and continued regular email updates about my health status from Atlanta which was sent to Ida and Bluffton and all over. Thank you. To the people of Atlanta helping and bringing more food than my family could eat, thank you. I'm sure the nurses at Grady Memorial Hospital in Atlanta appreciate that kind gesture as well from eating our leftovers.

To Zach Arend's father, who came and encouraged me immediately following the worst tragedy a parent can face, thank you. You are a man of courage and I do my best every day to honor Zach and all those killed.

To Hank Aaron, thank you for visiting. My parents have told me how much they enjoyed speaking with you and what a great man you were and how meaningful your conversations were. When we finally meet in heaven, we can talk baseball.

To my therapists, inpatient and outpatient, in dealing with me, thank you for positively impacting my life. To the band Rascal Flatts, I'm told you wanted to call me while I was in UTMC but didn't due to the fact I was not speaking yet. That's too bad we didn't get to speak but thank you! I love your music.

Thank you to Doctor Rock and Doctor Relm for believing in me from the first time I remember dealing with either of you. To the gorgeous young nurse in inpatient at UTMC, know you brought peace and hope to my new world of absolute chaos— thank you for being you. To the hospital social worker who helped my mom and me mentally and emotionally, thank you. To the neuropsychologist who gave me those dreadful test results, thank you for the motivation. From Bluffton, to Atlanta, to Ida, to Toledo and elsewhere, there are plenty of examples of pure human generosity and absolute brilliance. Speaking of brilliance, thank you to Trevor and Jim for fighting for me and your assistance in setting me up. Thank you also for being good men.

To the Ida community who sponsored a fundraiser and provided a great place to grow up, thank you. Still to this day, I am floored by all the signatures on my prayer quilt that a lady who lives in Ida made for me. That quilt is treasured, and I love reading the messages on it. To friends from Ida or Bluffton who supported me in their own way, thank you.

What the deep tissue therapeutic massage therapist did was tremendous. I guarantee that enormously helped, and may God bless you. Thank you to the National Wild Turkey Federation Whiteford chapter for giving a free turkey hunt. Then, after I got a turkey on that hunt, a local taxidermist stuffed and mounted it—for free. The mount is superb. That is unbeliev-able generosity at its best and thank you. To the softball player at Lourdes University who began the blood drive in honor of me, thank you. I wish I could accurately express what that did for me mentally and emotionally.

Lourdes University has my heart, and I will forever be grateful for what they did. I am convinced that, had it not been for Lourdes University, I would not be where I am today. Lourdes is where I first spoke with Ruthi about helping with this memoir. Without her input and skills, the completion of my manuscript would not have happened. To others also at Lour-des, who willingly helped throughout grad school and in other ways, thank you so much. Lourdes really was a perfect fit, and words do not even begin to capture how appreciative I feel for the opportunity you gave me. Attending Lourdes University was not about what they could get; the only thing Lourdes cared about was my success.

To my surviving teammates, I admire your courage to finish the rest of the season. I saw most of, if not all, your signatures on my prayer blanket or in my scrap book. Thank you for the support. To my friend, and head coach, James Grandey, I do not know how to adequately thank you for your impact on my life. I also do not know how to sufficiently express my admiration for what you had to deal with regarding the accident and keeping your head on straight. Hopefully you realize that your courage and drive continue to amaze and inspire me.

Speaking of awe and respect, thank you to my ESPN *E:60* feature writer and producer. It was a monumental project with the potential of impacting thousands of lives. Thank you, brother. You had my best interests at heart throughout the filming process, especially when I did not know what to expect, having never been on ESPN before. I am extremely grateful and hope you understand how much knowing you and calling you a friend means to me. You are my brother in Christ.

There have been countless kind gestures and words God has used to encourage me from many different people and I am sorry if I didn't mention you directly. All those events and people listed and I'm sure there are some not listed who had a tremendous impact and a mere "thank you" does not seem adequate in describing my gratitude. I'm sure I don't know every event or person that positively impacted life both before and after the accident but thank you from the bottom of my heart.

I certainly want to give a huge thank you and shout out to the one who is responsible for all the people and events in my life. My Lord and personal Savior, Jesus Christ. If it wasn't for what he had done, I would have no hope of recovering at all. There were times I could literally feel you were with me and helping me. Looking back at this entire journey, it's as if the Lord parted the sea and made things happen that many people and science says should not have happened. I have no words for an adequate thank you.

After reading some of these stories, my hope is that you can understand there were plenty of moments God was at work. Even after this horrific experience, I still believe in the goodness of God; I have witnessed and experienced it.

Finally, a big thank you goes out to my deceased teammates for being who you are. You were all quality young men on earth when you were taken from us, and I know I will see you again. Your lives will always be an inspiration to me, and we will forever be teammates. Please know that, for the remainder of my days on earth, I will be doing my best to honor you.

MEMORIAL

Along with other personal photos from key points during my journey, there is a photo of the sculpture at Memorial Field called "Circle of Remembrance" on my website myboyberta.-com. There are also pictures of the plaques dedicated to each of my teammates who were killed. "Circle of Remembrance" is at Memorial Field at Bluffton University.

NOTES

Dresser ride
https://www.youtube.com/watch?v=ZLiPU3NJv1o

ESPN feature
https://vimeo.com/52124340

CaringBridge website
https://www.caringbridge.org/visit/timberta

Personal website
myboyberta.com

ABOUT THE AUTHOR

This is Tim Berta's first book. After being involved with athletics in college, he has a passion for helping and inspiring youth in sports to be their best. The hope is to motivate anyone by telling his story of overcoming nearly impossible odds. After being given no chance by experts, he continues to live life on his own terms.

Tim is a member of the Lourdes University alumni board and a frequent speaker in high school or college classes, along with numerous other organizations. He works with student athletes at Lourdes University, is an occasional substitute teacher at a high school, and an assistant varsity Girl's golf coach at that same high school in Petersburg, Michigan.

When he is not writing or speaking, Tim enjoys golf, being out in nature, and exercise. You may contact him at myboyberta.com.